Kesiena Henry Esiri, Jr.

ORGANIZED RELIGION

What is wrong with today's Christianity?

N.B. All scriptures have been taken from The New King James Version of the Bible except otherwise stated.
ORGANIZED RELIGION

Copyright® Owner 2018 @ **Kesiena Henry Esiri, Jr.**
07035119795
Email: kesienahjr@gmail.com
Website: www.kesienaesiri.com

ISBN: 978-1-5136-3255-1

Published by
Holy Seed Network
08054895856

All right reserved. No Portion of this publication may be used without the express written consent of the publisher

Book Package by:
Babatee Prints @ 08037354933
johnmonica01@gmail.com

Book Cover Design by:
Jay Design Nigeria
jaydesign@gmail.com

To all those who have been "ruined" with hunger for a deeper experience with God; crying in the secret place for fresh fire on their lives so as to become authentic instruments in the hand of God. And to all those who have had questions in their hearts begging for answers but have continued in their various denominations; dissatisfied but "working for the Lord".
It is for you both I have written this and to you I humbly dedicate it.

Acknowledgement

I am a product of so many influences that I cannot mention all the men and women who have been of tremendous blessing to my life. In one way or the other they have shaped me into the man I have become today. It has been a rare priviledge to be a part of God's family. I am most grateful to God for the priviledged positions I have held in leading men. I realize that all I have become (and continue to become) has been by His tremendous outpour of grace, mercy and favour.

To all of you I say thank you.

A big thank you also to all the men and women of God who took time to read this before I published it; I am indebted to you for your invaluable input to this project. The work as it is today, is a product of your love and prayers.

I must however mention Pastor Ambrose Chiemeke my covenant brother and friend. Most of what I have written have been born out of the heartfelt discussions we have shared; special moments of dissecting revelations from the Word and igniting passion as we chewed on God's Word and His expectations for our lives as believers. Thank you for those days when we just talked and could feel God's manifest presence flood our conversations and for taking time out of your busy schedule to write the foreword of this book.

I am indebted to so many wonderful spiritual sons and daughters, friends and family that I would not attempt to name names lest I face the danger of leaving anyone out. I thank you for believing in God's call upon my life and encouraging me to pursue my convictions in God. May we continue to be a blessing one to another and may God richly favour you in life and ministry. However, two women I must mention for their immeasurable and overwhelming contributions and support at various stages of my life and ministry. Pastor Dr. Mrs. M. O Esiri (My mother) thank you so much for everything and taking time out of your busy schedule to read and edit the work. Weyinmi Tracy Esiri (My wife, covenant partner and friend) you know words will never be able to describe your immense support. Thank you for being my first congregation and believing in God's call on my life.

Finally, my uttermost praise and worship goes to God for His dealings with me in my walk with Him. Thank you Father for not leaving me to myself. My heavenly Father stripped my heart of all its excesses and brought me to a place where nothing but His full manifestation in my life would satisfy my deep cravings. Thank You Lord for constantly working on my life, keeping me hungry for You, and putting this message in my heart. Indeed, You have made my existence meaningful.

Contents

	Foreword
	Introduction
Chapter 1	Where Would I Rather Be?
Chapter 2	Religion – Why Not?
Chapter 3	Form But No Power!
Chapter 4	What Does It Mean To Work For God?
Chapter 5	Where Has Passion Gone?
Chapter 6	Wasted Existence
Chapter 7	Supernatural Generation
Chapter 8	What Now?

Foreword

> *"Religion frustrates and suffocates passion and if not stopped can waste a life."*
> *- Ambrose Chiemeke*

It is an honour and priviledge to write the Foreword of this timely and well thought out book, "Organized Religion." The truth contained therein cannot be overemphasized. Kesiena Esiri is one man with a burden for the kingdom. He's a rare gem in the Body of Christ and he's hugely imparted my life in more ways than one. Ours is a relationship that is simply 'made-in- heaven'. We have shared some deep spiritual moments that can only be divinely orchestrated. He has poured his pain and passion into this book that only the soul hungry for the supernatural will appreciate. You will be awakened from spiritual drudgery and slumber to the powerful and dynamic life in the Spirit as you go through the pages of this book.

I am yet to see a force that binds like religion. I fought and struggled with the shackles and frustrations of religion until I finally saw the light. Religion turns a man to a mere babe who never graduates from taking milk to strong meat, it impoverishes the total man. It leaves the man worse than it met him. Jesus said to the Scribes and Pharisees in Matthew 23:15 NLT "What sorrow awaits you teachers of religious law and you Pharisees. Hypocrites! For you cross land and sea to make one convert, and then you turn that person into twice the child of hell you yourselves are" Religion is a cyclical demon that erodes man's reason for existence. Napoleon Bonaparte succinctly puts it thus: "Religion is excellent stuff for keeping common people quiet."

Worse still, religion negates the intentions and expectations of God. The apostle Paul clearly captures God's expectations in Ephesians 4:12-13 AMP "His intention was the perfecting and the full equipping of the saints (His consecrated people), that they should do the work of ministering toward building up Christ's body (the church), That it might develop until we all attain oneness in the faith and in the comprehension of the full and accurate knowledge of the Son of God, that we might arrive at really mature manhood (the completeness of personality which is nothing less than the standard height of Christ's own perfection), the measure of the stature of the fullness of the Christ and the completeness found in Him." What more can truly satisfy the heart of a father than to see his children maturing to perfection? I join in the plea with the writer that we should go back to God and that very quickly. How can we not see the light?

Kesiena Esiri in this book by the grace of God has been able to tear to shreds the evil covering of religion. This book will help drive away the falsehood religion has infested the church with and set her free to fulfil her purpose. The message of the kingdom builds rather than stunt the man. Acts 20:32 KJV "And now, brethren, I commend you to God, and to the word of his grace, which is able to build you up, and to give you an inheritance among all them which are sanctified." Can we not see that there is no other way to spiritual growth except through the Word? Can we not learn from the Christians in Berea how they searched the Scriptures daily whether the things they heard in the synagogue agree with the Word of God? (Acts 17:10-12).

"Organized Religion" captures the real issues in today's Christianity that we cannot afford to dismiss it with a wave of the hand. I dare say that God is not getting enough returns on His investment in our lives due to religiosity. Religion numbs and incapacitates the man thereby limiting and binding him to a set of legalistic rules that will never do him any good. In a world where people are fast becoming the means rather than the object of our Christian vocation, the relevance of this book can never be overemphasized. This book is an eye opener and I humbly recommend it to every soul that desires to grow into the full stature of Christ. This book will set you loose, it will transform you as your mind is renewed; as no true transformation can happen without first of all a mental renewal.

It is quite tragic when lives are patterned after a lie. It does not matter what you do for a lie, you can even die for it but a lie is at best a lie. This book is a wakeup call to the church, especially the church in my country, Nigeria. If we want our impact to be truly felt in all nooks and crannies of this nation it is time we embrace the truth, the whole truth and nothing but the truth. "A lie is a lie even if everybody believes it. The truth is the truth even if nobody believes it." - David Stevens

■Ambrose C. Chiemeke is a Pastor with the RCCG.

Introduction

This book and its title I am afraid might win me more antagonists and critics than friends. However, I hope all who read it realize that in writing I speak to myself also. Like Steve Hill said in his book "Spiritual Avalanche", *"As you're reading and something is said that offends or you feel does not relate to you, always remember, possibly millions are reading or listening to this visionary book. What may seem irrelevant to you could be shaking the spiritual foundation of someone else. Relax and keep reading. The Lord has something to say to everyone"*.

Those who have gone way ahead of me might seek to be on the defensive and utterly reject this work by reading with a closed mind while those who are in my generation would agree with most of what I would share but may never have the courage to publicly affirm it. I hope with this book, both groups of this divide will arise and act as God through His Spirit will stir them to and not as their minds will suggest. This book hasn't been written to slight anyone or gain popularity. These are words that attempt to give form to the pain in my heart and the cries I hear from the realms. I relate with these words penned by Tozer for it gives form to the inexpressible in my heart - *"The sight of the languishing church around me and the operations of a new spiritual power within me have set up a pressure impossible to resist. Whether or not the book ever reaches a wide public, it still has to be written if for no other reason than to relieve an unbearable burden on my heart".*

There is something wrong with Christianity as we know it today. We bear some semblance with the generations of Christians who existed before us the only harrowing difference being the portentous lack of spiritual power. E.M. Bounds a Christian from generations past said *"The individual Christian must be lifted to a higher plane of personal experience, personal devotion and influence. He must be so charged with spiritual forces, that others will be affected by his presence and touch"*. Sadly, personal experience, personal devotion and influence are not the areas of emphasis in today's Christianity. Is it then a surprise that we seem to have "grown", become more structured and organized when compared to the days of men like E.M. Bounds yet we are seeing less (if any at all) of the manifestations of the power of God? Christians today seem to have no influence whatsoever over the societies in which they live. The world is not affected by our presence or touch. The average believer does not live beyond and above the natural. Invariably because we are not charged with spiritual forces enough to bring any meaningful impact.

Religion and religious people have flooded the Christian

sphere. There are so many things we do in present day Christianity that either has no value or is a complete waste of time. Andy Stanley said, *"Where religion has taken first place, leaders become self-righteous while followers become hypocrites."* What we see in present day is leaders coming up with rules and more rules; dumping these traditions and rituals on the followers and the followers must pretend like they are comfortable and following the rules. Our church auditoriums have become full of hypocrites; people who are one thing in church but another thing entirely soon as they are out of our buildings. In fact, most people today cannot wait to get out of our church buildings because it seems it is only when they are out of there, they can truly experience freedom.

I have been burdened with so many questions – why does it seem like we pray so fervently both in the open and secret and yet we produce so little results? So many good Christians when sick and dying have prayed or confessed God's Word over their lives and yet if they had not taken steps to buy drugs or run to the doctor, they probably would have died. How come there is so much activity in the Christian sphere but we are producing so little supernatural results? Why is there so much demand for money in Christendom today? Emphasis is placed on things like tithes, prophet offerings and seed faith while our pews are full of impoverished and sick people. In spite of the obvious aberration starring us in the face, we continue to gather day-in, day-out without any meaningful change happening in the lives of the people we gather. One or two testimonies and we are satisfied but the larger crowd is still sick, crippled and languishing in poverty. Some of you would have met people who have been "serving God" for 30 years yet their lives have no proof that God is indeed what He says He is in His Word. Some are giving tithes, seed faith and prophet offerings but ending up worse off. We cannot relate between the poor widow who gives tithes and the preacher who has no secular job, feeds off the church offerings and yet lives lavishly; lacking no "good thing". We have bigger churches, larger programmes and events but an insignificant number of Christians truly making impact on the world. Can a man be connected to God and still be irrelevant in the world? Why should I go on doing something that seems like a complete waste of time? How can I be part of God's family and yet be "suffering"? These issues seriously bother my heart and there are no words to describe the extent of dissatisfaction I feel.

It seems to me, that this is the same "place" Gideon was in his own life when he asked the angel of God "If indeed God is with us, why have all these things befallen us? And where are all the miracles our fathers told us of, saying, did the Lord not bring us out of Egypt?" Judges 6:13. When we compare the Christianity of today and its associated results with the Christianity of old we can only wonder where is God? If indeed He is with us like we say He is then something definite has gone wrong. Gideon concluded in that verse of scripture "but now the Lord has forsaken us and delivered us into the hands of the Midianites" Invariably, he was saying, for us to be where we are, it must be that God has forsaken us. If He hasn't, we would not be having this kind of results. I sincerely can relate with Gideon here because we are having the exact same experience in the church today. So much noise, activity and propaganda but very little (most times insignificant) results.

I took time to engage God in prayer while I also watched the happenings in the church across Africa. It was then I discovered the malaise that has caused this anomaly. The "disease" is what I have called in this book, "Organized Religion". This phrase I use in the book to represent the religious establishment, religious traditions or religious order of present day Christianity. It continues to ravage the church and I believe if not reined in/confronted urgently, would utterly "damage" us.

When we should be on our faces weeping for the true manifestation of God in our midst, we are comfortable with larger auditoriums, fatter offerings, "little successes" and plenty of wasteful activity.

We now have rituals, doctrines and laws in the church that enslave people instead of making them true believers. These rituals have also taken it a step further to oil the "machineries" of our organizations such that we can go on for years without even noticing that the Holy Spirit is not in our midst. We have completely neglected the place and ministry of the Holy Spirit. All is well as long as we have fuller auditoriums, schools, fat bank accounts and some recognition from the world.

What bothers me the most in all of this is the fact that as Christians instead of us being sad and worried, on the contrary we are happy and comfortable with the abnormal situation we find ourselves. I believe this "ungodly" state of false security and satisfaction, more than anything else has contributed to the continued lack of supernatural manifestation in large degrees in our denominations. When people who should be pilgrims have begun to build permanent monuments where they are temporary residents it is a sign that we have lost the essence/core of who we are.

The pattern of life shown by Jesus Christ, the apostles and saints of old clearly emphasizes the core aspect of Christianity yet we amble on limply without seeking to become what they became that we might do what they did. Dear reader, Christianity is about influence. If we would realize this, then we would do everything we can to ensure we bring the influence of God to our World. Jesus began His ministry by saying *"The Kingdom of heaven is at hand..."* Mathew 4:17. *"Now after that John was put in prison, Jesus came into Galilee, preaching the gospel of the kingdom of God"* Mark 1:14. *"Jesus answered, My kingdom is not of this world..."* John 18:36. It seems to me that Jesus came announcing the arrival of influence from a greater kingdom. He proved this influence with signs and wonders. The church in this generation has become comfortable being the lamp of the church when we should be the light of the world. We have so much comfort in church but no influence on the world. The "disease" called organized religion has brought us to this place and lulled us to a comfortable but fatal sleep.

In the pages of this book, you will find some of the things and issues I have identified as part of the "disease" and what I believe the church in our generation needs to do (and do fast) to cure us all. I know I might not have mentioned all root causes of the current lack of influence in Christendom but I trust that with the little principles we identify herein, we can hope for a glorious end. This writer hopes to challenge everyone who is a believer to rise and change the trend. Just like Gideon did after he had an encounter with the angel of the Lord.

In the pages of this book, I have attempted to confront issues we are told to be silent about but seems to be creating an atmosphere of falsehood around our faith. Too many genuine believers have chosen the so-called path of honour – that instead of confront what seemingly we cannot change, it is better to die in silence. I sincerely hope after reading the truths shared herein, our disposition surely will change.

I do not speak in these pages as one who has attained but I empty my heart as God has filled it in the periods leading up to writing this book. A man I have grown to deeply admire and respect A.W Tozer said *"to speak to men in the name of God is a priviledge possible to us only through the grace of our Lord Jesus Christ"*. I have made this quote a guiding light for my journey in ministry and as such do not take the opportunity of writing this book for granted believing that He who made this possible will also cause a flame to be lit in the souls of them that read it. All I ask, is that it be read with an open heart believing that he who wrote did so by grace!

The only qualifications I bring to these pages is a genuine heart of love and passion for God, His people and His work upon the earth pending His return. I do not lay claim to any degrees from any theological seminary. My goal is to provoke the ardent reader and church member to seek God as the thoughts I share herein have provoked me to seek Him with great crying and hunger.

I desire that those who are already in our family (the family of God's children) and even those yet unborn might truly be free to live in the fullness of what our Father has made available to us here on earth. *"The Lord Jesus has come to take from us every yoke of bondage and to set us free to serve Him in freshness and spontaneity of the Spirit, and all this by the simple sight of Him which the Holy Spirit gives to the eye of faith"* – Roy and Revel Hession

My sincere prayers go with this book and with everyone who will "defy the odds" to read it. May you see Jesus as God fills your heart with His love; and may your contributions to His family here on earth do a lot of good and no harm.

Stay rapturable!

Pastor Kesiena Esiri

Where Would I Rather Be?

"And let us not neglect our meeting together, as some people do, but encourage one another, especially now that the day of his return is drawing near." Hebrews 10:25 NLT

"To live within the religious family does not mean we must approve of everything that is done there"
- A.W. Tozer

Before I dive into the things set in my heart, I would love to correct certain impressions that may be formed as you read the next chapters of this book.

I am a firm believer in the gathering of the saints. I believe that what we call the church (our buildings where we gather) is a wonderful tool in not only reaching out to the lost but also in helping to shape the lives of men that gather there regularly. Like A.A. Allen puts it, "Find a good church home, where God's Word is taught and believed, where the power of God is present and welcome, where God is confirming His Word with signs following, and where God's people speak the things which become sound doctrine. Then make it a practice to be present whenever God and His people meet".

Notice the striking aspects of what "a good church home" should look like as I have highlighted above. This is what it should be – God's Word is taught (the genuine gospel and not "selfish doctrines" is preached), God is visibly present, His Words spoken by our preachers are confirmed with signs and wonders following, and God's people speak sound doctrine. If indeed we can find such a place in this generation, then we must make it a practice to be present whenever God and His people meet. For if all these that A.A Allen mentions are present, then one can be confident that God indeed will be present in our churches. The sad thing though is that not many of us can look at our churches and agree that these things we speak of are actually present.

But where shall we go?
I remember in 1999 when I was admitted into the university in Delta State, Nigeria, I was a born-again believer and member of a church family. My mum had raised us in the way of the Lord and in the time that passed, she also grew to become an ordained pastor in the church family where we belonged. Despite this wonderful spiritual atmosphere around my life, I had issues (like most people do) and was working towards perfection when I arrived in school. I found myself in a constant battle with temptation and eventually succumbed to some vices. I didn't just

put my hands up and abandon God though; I had one leg out in the world and the other in church. Then came this faithful day, I was sitting out in front of my lecture hall waiting for the lecturer when I noticed a brother walk past me. He had gone about fifteen feet away from me when he suddenly stopped and turned back towards me. Up till today I still do not understand why I was watching this brother but somehow my eyes were fixed on him. He got to me and said "God said to come talk with you". In my heart, I sighed "All these religious people at it again" but he continued... Asked if I was born-again (I said yes obviously) and he went ahead to invite me to fellowship and I obliged. And the rest like they say "Is history".

I don't want to go into further details but that singular act of getting me to join the meeting of God's family on campus went a long way to shaping me for God's call and ministry assignment. Fast forward to 2003 and it was in the same family the fiery passion and deep longing for God began to build and I found myself answering the call to ministry. Bottom line is, if I had forsaken the gathering of God's people I probably would have been lost forever. There were bible teachings that shaped me, relationships that inspired me and God-encounters that "ruined" me for good; I never could be satisfied with nominal Christianity after some of my encounters on campus. Part of me knew there was more to God and I determined to experience deeper levels before I die.

Getting people out of the assembly has been a major tool of the devil and to demand that the church be "dis-banded" is to subtly assist the gates of hell in prevailing. This is not the goal with this book - not by any chance!

The gathering of the people of God have been a tremendous blessing to me and many others. To take the opportunity away would be to join hands with our greatest enemy; the devil.

The moral of it all is that we need the church; period! Without her we all would be in trouble. A wise man put it this way "While each child is born separate from the rest, it is born into a family and after that must live in the fellowship of the rest of the household. And the man who comes to Christ in the loneliness of personal repentance and faith is also born into a family. The Church is called the household of God and it is the ideal place to rear young Christians. Just as a child will not grow up to be a normal adult if forced to live alone, so the Christian who withdraws from the fellowship of other Christians will suffer great soul injury as a result. Such a one can never hope to develop normally"

If our Christian development would be practical and normal, then we must not forsake the fellowship of the brethren. However, a crisis then arises when the fellowship becomes a channel for creating "abnormal Christians".

As the writer of Hebrews mentions, we must not neglect the assembly of the brethren; as the NLT version puts it, we must not neglect our meeting together especially now that the day of our Saviour's return is drawing near. I particularly like how it is translated in the Holman Christian Bible "not staying away from our worship meetings, as some habitually do, but encouraging each other, and all the more as you see the day drawing near."

The key with this verse is not just the gathering, it is in the "why" of the meeting. Our meetings are to be for worship and to encourage one another. But the correct platform is being used for the wrong purposes. When the place of meeting has been turned into a place of "indoctrination" then a problem exists. When the place of encouragement has become a place where men and women are held bound like modern day slaves then we are in trouble. One of my many instructors in the faith describes this as being in charismatic zoos.

It seems to me that the writer of Hebrews is pointing out to us that we must be deliberate in how we gather. The gathering cannot be for religious entertainment or to feed the ego of any man but for worship of the Father and fellowship of the saints.

For example, someone leaves one denomination to join another for whatever reason and shows proof of baptism by immersion which is the correct doctrine of scripture yet the new denomination insists "if you would be a member of our church you must be baptized again." Where did all this come from? When denominations begin to insist on baptizing people twice for membership sake even though we have no scriptural backing for this I think there is a problem. Part of the problem is; most people know denominational doctrines but have little or no knowledge of bible doctrines. If a man really knows what baptism by immersion means, he would not want to baptize people twice.

Too much "evil" is being done in the name of religion. I have met so many broken and hurting individuals who have been damaged not by the enemy without but the wolf within; badly burnt by religion and religious activity. We are more organized, we have very large gatherings, and we are breaking records almost every year; we seem to be making so much progress, but we are not seeing a commensurate impact in the lives of the people or the fabric of the communities in which we live. I think this is something that should greatly disturb any true child of God.

We focus on denominational doctrines instead of teaching young and old believers alike the basic doctrines of the bible. The problem is, one enslaves while the latter liberates and empowers. So, the results we see in our denominations are pointers to what we are actually putting across to those who sit in our pews week-in, week-out.

Most Christians cannot tell you what salvation means. They have no understanding of atonement, redemption, righteousness, justification, the new creation and other basic bible doctrines. These have been replaced (especially in the Nigerian church) with demonology, battle against "witchcraft delay" and deliverance from strange powers, prophetic declarations, anointing for breakthroughs and the chase for miracles. So instead of using the platform correctly, we abuse the priviledge and "corrupt" the minds of God's children. We celebrate these things as "new revelations" but we forget that Apostle Paul clearly admonishes that every man must be careful how he builds on the foundation that has been laid for every man will give account. 1 Corinthians 3:10-13

The result?
Weak, sick, shallow and unprepared believers. The day of our Saviour's return is near yet we are grossly unprepared. The inner experiences of these so-called church ministers, workers and members are so shallow it would make the saints who have gone ahead shake their heads in disbelief. When a member of God's family has more faith in the picture of the general overseer of their denomination than the Word of God it tells me there is a crisis. When people are made to feel like they are sinning against God because they cannot travel long hours for a program in another state or city then I fear that there is a problem. When how much you have or earn becomes the yardstick for where you sit or

which position you hold in church then I fear God might be weeping.

I am worried that what we call sowing and reaping might in God's eyes be exploiting the poor. We continue to give, give and give and yet our family members (Church members) are impoverished. Targets are set in church like it is some business organization. One only needs to hear the figures being mentioned to wonder why we demand so much. I dare us to be honest with ourselves. Some of the projects we have embarked on, some of the financial demands we have made on the children of this family who actually sent us? Our egos or our Father? If indeed we have learnt how to tap into God's resources for life and ministry the outlook of the church towards "sowing and reaping" would change.

We are being destroyed not from without but from within and I fear that what we call progress might in God's eyes be nothing but organized religion. The letter kills but it is the Spirit that gives life as Paul clearly points out in 2 Corinthians 3:6. People are hungry for deeper experiences but I fear that we are giving out dead sermons, dead ideologies, dead doctrines and dead prophecies. I have tried to imagine where a soul hungry for God can go in this generation. You might be desiring God so deeply and crying in your heart for a deeper experience but when you walk into our church buildings, all you would hear would in no way feed your hungry soul. The messages from the pulpits these days leave me wondering where the man who desires an encounter with God can go to find Him. People leave our gatherings worse than they came and yet with our adverts and billboards we demand that they come again the very next week, month or year. The sound has been made that the arrival of the bridegroom is imminent but our focus has still not shifted to the preparing of the brethren. When we should be leading men into personal encounters with the Great One we are busy taking them on the road of fear or motivation for personal success and prosperity. I fear that many gatherings (some very large with what we call "results") God will query; for in them He had no place nor pleasure.

Yet again I am forced to remind us that my goal in writing all this is not to point fingers. After all I am part of God's body. If I choose to sit on my "high horse" to point fingers, then I am of all men most miserable for fingers also point at me. I am hoping that we stop, ponder and act accordingly. I am desiring that the words on these pages provoke you to prayer, intercession and passion for authentic Christianity. We who read this must first be revived before we can cause revival to spread in our denominations.

I am not asking that we stop gathering. I am asking that we become deliberate in ensuring that why and how we gather achieves God's purpose.

This unique platform the writer of Hebrews says is for us to worship, fellowship and encourage the brethren. Jesus said, "The words that I speak to you they are spirit and life..." John 6:63. When men leave our gatherings they should not leave empty, hungry or feeling defeated. Instead the Word from the pulpit must set free, encourage, uplift and empower. People should leave church sure they just heard God speak. When the focus after a church meeting is on how eloquent or powerful the man of God is/was then I fear, the people gathered to meet man and not the Father – God. When the focus after leaving a church meeting is fear because of how powerful and marauding the devil and his agents are, then I fear that the people gathered to hear a hireling and not the Good Shepherd.

Let the focus of our worship services be God and not man. If we must develop doctrines for our denominations let the focus not be the denominational doctrine but the bible. Let our goal grow beyond creating denominational individuals but true children of God. Discipleship isn't about creating a church member but developing a mature child of God. Our emphasis has got to change.

In prayer, our emphasis has got to change! When Christians pray these days, it is almost as if priority has shifted from God and is now focused on the devil. The devil now seemingly takes credit for everything that happens in the life of the child of God. So, without even knowing it, we have begun to give the devil such glory and relevance that he should not normally enjoy. The devil doesn't deserve this recent hype; we have overhyped the devil and made him unnecessarily popular such that after our prayer meetings our people are thinking more of demons than God. You sure have noticed what I speak about here.

So where would I rather be? Do I abandon the church and stay at home? No way! Too many people have flung their hands up in the air in disgust and hopelessness and eventually turned their backs on anything that looks like the gathering of God's children. However, this is not what God wants from us. Any student of church history will tell you that most of the revolutionary steps that have shaped and birth the church as we know it today, came at a heavy price. Men and women fired up by the Holy Spirit simply refused to accept the status quo and were willing to die for what they believed was the correct approach. Today and in this generation, we are in dire need of such men and women again! Some of which are reading this book right now. It is time for a reformation-restoration movement in the church especially the Nigerian church.

Like Tozer said and I quoted at the beginning of this chapter, that to live within the religious family does not mean we must approve of all that happens therein. However, to not approve and be silent amounts to approval. So, we must begin to use the "little" platforms God has given us to bring the desired change. Are you a Sunday School teacher? Are you the Senior Pastor of a church? Are you a church worker? Are you the General Overseer of a ministry? Then start from where you are. Our emphasis must return to the things that matter to God. We cannot afford to give organized religion the chance to damage what God has prepared for them who love Him. It is time to arise and not only demand change but contribute to making change happen.

Though I cannot remember where I read it or who wrote it, love this quote:

"Without the soul divinely quickened and inspired, the observances of the grandest ritualism are as worthless as the motions of a galvanized corpse."

If I have not stirred a flame in your heart yet, I hope to do so with the discourse in the next chapters. Also, I may have "angered" you with my conclusions here but I do hope you will oblige me and continue reading. I warn you though the next chapters do not spare "religion" and "religious activity."

Please do read on.

RELIGION - WHY NOT?

*When religion has said its last word,
there is little that we need other than God Himself*
– A.W Tozer

*I fear that what we call Christianity today
is all religious activity with no roots in true spirituality.
Religion is a spirit and if not reined in now might destroy
all that we have laboured for over the centuries*
– K. H Esiri

*What one generation tolerates,
the next generation will embrace.*
– John Wesley

*There seems to be such a clutch for self-promotion, self-labeling,
self-advertisement and self-possession.
That is very dangerous because the commission God gave
the church is not to promote itself but to reach the world.
Also, the world is being given a very distorted picture
of the true message of the kingdom.*
– Myles Munroe

When I read the bible, one thing that strikes me especially in the New Testament is the simplicity with which Christ can be found. Sometimes the expectations from God for His children are put across so simply that one asks "can this be true?" We find ourselves in this internal struggle because of the religious complexity that now plagues our generation. There seems to be a "secret code" suggesting that if it is not hard it cannot be God. The simplicity we see as Jesus progresses from infanthood to maturity, as the apostles of old are baptized in the Holy Spirit and begin to bear witness of the Messiah, and as Paul's revelations pour forth in his letters to the church seem to have been replaced with organizations, structures, programmes and a frenzy of activity that most of the time leave the famished souls of kingdom citizens more and more hungry for a genuine deeper experience. Sadly, some die without ever really enjoying these deep dimensions or realities of God.

Most people are turning away from organized religion because with every meeting in sanctuary buildings the more emptiness they feel inside. Could this be why we are seeing less and less of young people turning to Christ as against a large number leaving the church? There are lots of stories of big name preachers in America whose wards/children have turned away from the Church and given themselves wholly to satan and the god of entertainment. In Nigeria, the story is not too different. It is a popular saying amongst believers that "Children of preachers are the most corrupt and sinful". Even though I believe these young people ultimately are responsible for their decisions, I cannot totally absolve Christendom of responsibility. We have since stopped preaching the simplicity of the cross and its associated sacrifices and turned to entertainment, comedy and "music" to get our pews full and at the same time enslaving these young people with doctrines, dogma and denominational rules. Why stay in the sanctuary enslaved with religion when I can be in the world, have the same entertainment, comedy and "music" and above all be "free"? I think the strength of the argument is with the latter.

I am worried that Christian leaders have completely misunderstood God's instruction to influence the world. We gather hundreds and thousands of people in buildings and call this success when the whole world around us decays and perishes before our very eyes. We focus on indoctrinating men instead of building true Christians of influence; so, we do more and more programmes, gather in large conventions or camp meetings, celebrate testimonies within our buildings and yet the world around us crumbles. Governments are corrupt, poverty continues to ravage people including those who help bank roll our ministries, we are seeing less and less of miracles and world influence when compared to the generations before us, yet we carry on because we have replaced the simplicity of the gospel with the complexity of organized religion in the name of Christianity.

As Myles Munroe put it, *"Right now religion is the number one problem in the world and we know that all the terrorism that we are experiencing, and the fear is mostly motivated by religion. Jesus Christ did not bring a religion into the world. He brought a kingdom. The world doesn't need another religion. It doesn't need traditions and rituals. The world needs a practical application of principles and precepts that will impact their daily lives. Jesus said blessed are those who are poor spiritually for to them belong, not a religion, but the kingdom of heaven. Only the kingdom satisfies spiritual hunger—not religion"*

Little wonder, the world no longer takes us seriously because when you meet the average Christian on the street all they talk about is I belong to this ministry or that ministry, I am a member of that denomination or that society, this is what my Pastor, Bishop, Apostle or Vicar said but their lives pale in comparism when put side by side with the expectations stated clearly in scriptures. It seems like mere child's play when compared to those who lived the Christian life generations before ours. Can we truly stand side by side with those who have gone ahead? I leave that for Christian leaders in this generation to answer.

I am deeply saddened that we think we have made Christianity more organized but I fear that what we currently celebrate as growth and expansion is just organized religion. The danger with religion is that it enslaves, corrupts and produces people with no true depth. It has form but lacks power; we have people who talk the talk but have shallow personal experiences with God. Our pews are full of religious people who know doctrines but have no inner experience with God; no deep relationship with Christ.

They talk about a God they have no practical personal experience of. There is a crisis in Christendom and if we don't reel it in fast we are in danger of raising a generation who will not know God. They will know the name of their general overseers, the rules, doctrines and codes of conducts of their ministries, the dates for conventions and annual meetings, and the number of countries where their ministries are thriving but would not know what it means to truly pursue and apprehend God; to get to the place where they too can experience what Peter, Paul and other apostles experienced that they were willing to die for Jesus! An author describing the saints of old said, they went to the stake to be burned to death like men going to a wedding feast. Theses saints; men like John Wycliffe went to the stake to be burnt to death with a smile and a song of worship on their lips. What would happen inside a man that would make him so passionate about God that He recklessly abandons his life in His hands? Surely not religion or religious activity but a deep, continuous, personal engagement with God that translates into a lifelong love relationship.

Christ did not die to start a religion. Christ was born, lived and died to make it possible for man to be restored into genuine relationship with the Father-God. The church in my generation with her programs, activities and desire for glory have inadvertently (sometimes intentionally) distorted the message painting the wrong picture for men to see.

Are we surprised at the recent upsurge in charlatans that now have "successful" ministries? There seems to be a steady proliferation of prophets and apostles in Nigeria and make no mistake about it dear preacher, most of your members attend the programmes these con-men organize. They go to them because we have enslaved them with doctrines but not fed their famishing souls. When the storms of life come, they have no depth because we have not told them the truth about the cross. They run from one prayer house to the other seeking deliverance from one demon or the other because all you have told them has done nothing but excite the flesh. They go to these con-men because when compared to those of us who claim to be real, these men have more "results" than us. We have shown them what is possible but have produced little or no results to validate our speaking. They go to these representatives of the devil manifesting as angels of light because they have more results than those of us who claim to be the "real men of God". We have told them God can heal but they have watched us tacitly avoid praying for the crippled and those in wheel chairs in our midst. They have seen us celebrate their "falling under the anointing" while they struggle in their hearts with the reality that when they got off the floor, they didn't experience anything tangible and nothing in their lives changed. They go back to be the same "old" person they were yet we are being celebrated as anointed men of God.

Visit any bible teaching sanctuary on the days of bible study or prayer meetings and it will not surprise you to see how only few men are willing to come and be taught the truth of the gospel. We have told our people that to be taught the truths of the cross are no longer necessary all they need do is name it and claim it. We have taught them that soon as they see our faces we would prophesy, and all would be well. So, they continue looking for the next popular prophetic face, so they can have some peace and joy in their lives. People are hungry, and we have fed them "rotten tomatoes". We have enslaved the sheep of Jesus with a corrupt Christianity that can only be described as organized religion.

The sad thing is, the hunger for genuine spiritual truth and tangible experiences in God is deep in the land. Christians are hungry, but the reality now is, it is so hard to find a place where the light of His Spirit shines and bread is broken to feed the famished soul. Very few platforms in our nation have given voice to the one crying in the wilderness "make straight the ways and paths of the Lord". Time after time, I listen to the frustrations on the hearts of many Christians in Nigeria and my heart bleeds. Oh God, visit our nation again! The hunger in the land is overwhelming.

I listened to a man of God speak on the frustrations of the Christian faith in Nigeria and he raised questions that even our church leaders are afraid to confront. The frustrations of unanswered prayers and the frustration of the seemingly powerlessness of the Word of God when confronted with real life situations. In Nigeria, we have all manner of prayer sessions, we claim we teach our people God's Word but in the midst of all these frenzied activities we roll out year on end we do not have commensurate results. There seem to be no true evidence in the lives of the people. Our auditoriums and buildings are still packed full, but the people are frustrated! Why? Because we have not taught the people how to have personal encounters with God. Majority of Christians in Nigeria have not seen or experienced Jesus for themselves. All they know are doctrines on how to be a good church member.

To the believer who would read the chapters in this book, like I say to those whom God by His grace has given me the priviledge to teach over the years, "Please know God for yourself". You need to spend time with the Word, you need to desire a personal encounter with God that will shape your Christian walk. You cannot run your relationship with Christ based on another man's experience. If you find where the unadulterated Word is being taught with all simplicity and liberty, then stay put and ensure you grow. The easiest way to find out if where you are is right for you is the freedom you feel; the preacher isn't trying to say "the right things" to keep you neither is he saying things to you for his personal benefit but all you hear is the truth. Then you will begin to see results daily as you put to work the things being taught.

Organized religion focuses on "doing" but true Christianity focuses on "being". There is a continued emphasis on service for God; the machinery within our church walls are so oiled that even without the presence of the Holy Spirit things will go on as normal and we would not even notice. We focus now on performance while our Christian life suffers. The true man which is spirit is lean and suffering but emphasis has been placed on what we can do for God instead of who we are to become as He meets us on a personal level. Jesus personally had to address this matter in the house of Lazarus. Martha was in a frenzy to serve and make food and noticed that Mary instead chose to sit at the feet of Jesus. She complained to Jesus asking Him to get Mary to join her, but our Savior reminded her that one thing was needful and Mary had chosen the right path; to sit at the foot of the Master and learn of Him. Mary chose rather to feed her famished soul with the words tumbling out of the King of Glory's mouth.

"Now while they were on their way, it occurred that Jesus entered a certain village, and a woman named Martha received and welcomed Him into her house. And she had a sister named Mary, who seated herself at the Lord's feet and was listening to His teaching. But Martha [overly occupied and too busy] was distracted with much serving; and she came up to Him and said, Lord, is it nothing to You that my sister has left me to serve alone? Tell her then to help me [to lend a hand and do her part along with me]! But the Lord replied to her by saying, Martha, Martha, you are anxious and troubled about many things; There is need of only one or but a few things. Mary has chosen the good portion [that which is to her advantage], which shall not be taken away from her". Luke 10:38-42 AMP.

Organized Religion places a somewhat fanatical emphasis on giving and honouring spiritual leaders to the sad decline of true apostolic Christianity. In our churches today, the emphasis on tithes or giving gifts/money to "spiritual uplines" is heart wrenching for people like me. I hear preachers scream at the top of their voices that anyone who does not tithe is a thief and since all thieves will go to hell, the non-tither will also go to hell. Beloved, regardless of how nice this sounds or theologically acceptable it seems, it cannot be validated by scripture or proved in the furnace of true heartfelt prayer to God. You might ask well sir, what about Malachi chapter 3? The "Holy Grail" if you will of the tithing doctrine. Well, since I suspect that is on your mind, let us examine scriptures:

Even from the days of your fathers ye are gone away from mine ordinances, and have not kept them. Return unto me, and I will return unto you, saith the Lord of hosts. But ye said, Wherein shall we return? <u>*Will a man rob God? Yet ye have robbed me. But ye say, Wherein have we robbed thee? In tithes and offerings.*</u> *Ye are cursed with a curse: for ye have robbed me, even this whole nation. Bring ye all the tithes into the storehouse, that there may be meat in mine house, and prove me now herewith, saith the Lord of hosts, if I will not open you the windows of heaven, and pour you out a blessing, that there shall not be room enough to receive it. And I will rebuke the devourer for your sakes, and he shall not destroy the fruits of your ground; neither shall your vine cast her fruit before the time in the field, saith the Lord of hosts. And all nations shall call you blessed: for ye shall be a delightsome land, saith the Lord of hosts.* Mal 3:7-12

Notice the portion I have underlined in the text. The Lord said, "you have robbed me in tithes and offerings". First thing you should ask is, since the man who does not tithe is labelled a thief in modern day Christianity based on this scripture, then the man who does not give offerings should also be called a thief because the bible says, "IN TITHES AND OFFERINGS". The question then becomes, have you ever heard your pastor in your local assembly call the man who does not give offering a thief? I can bet that you have not. Why do preachers only emphasize tithing? Because that's the one with a fixed percentage and probably offers greater returns to fuel ambitions, feed bank accounts and create a steady stream of wealth. With offerings, they cannot dictate how much you give so they leave it be. If the preachers say the non-tither is a thief, then by all means the non-giver of offerings is also a thief. But because they know they cannot validate this by scripture, offerings are not mentioned in the "thief going to hell" doctrine as relates to tithes. Beloved, you will see that the spirit driving *religion* in modern day is the spirit of covetousness and greed. Although, certain denominations engage in these things out of ignorance and tradition not necessarily greed.

Some churches I know teach that if on your way to church to pay your tithe you discover someone in need and decide to help and end up spending the tithe, you are still owing God tithe and must pay it with a percentage increase using Leviticus 27:31 as their premise for this erroneous teaching. There is no way this is correct by scripture. The one-time tithes are mentioned in the gospels, we see Jesus point out that tithing though good was not as weighty before God as other things like mercy, justice and faithfulness.

Woe unto you, scribes and Pharisees, hypocrites! <u>for ye pay tithe of mint and anise and cummin</u>, and <u>have omitted the weightier matters of the law, judgment, mercy, and faith</u>: these ought ye to have done, and not to leave the other undone. Mathew 23:23.

You have left the weightier masters of the law like mercy... Some Christians today, even if they see their neighbor's child dying and they have their tithe at home, they will rather hold on to the tradition of taking the tithe to their local assembly on Sunday morning while they watch the child die. Because, the teaching in denominations today, say that, if you use that money for that child, you are still owing God tithe. How can this be true? There is no way we can validate this by scriptures. Also, Jesus gave us the parable of the "Good Samaritan" where a wounded and helpless Jewish man was ignored by the priest and Levite only to be attended to by a Samaritan who by reason of culture should have no dealings with Jews and ended that parable by saying "Go and do likewise" See Luke 10:25-37. This shows where the heart of the Father-God is.

I beg you dear reader, push emotionalism and sentimentalism aside, take the high road of honor like the Berean Christians and search under the guidance of the Holy Spirit the scriptures to see if these things I raise here are true.

Notice that even in the same verse above, what the Pharisees tithed were herbs/spices – mint, anise (also called dill in some translations) and cumin. There was no tithing of money! And this was not because the Pharisees were farmers or shepherds and had no income. Remember who paid Judas Iscariot thirty pieces of silver? These men had money, but tithed herbs/spices used for flavouring food or in some cases as medicine for treating stomach ailments. The question one should ask is why?

The tithe was God's way of providing for His sons the priests as part of the covenant relationship of the priesthood. Read the scripture below carefully...with emphasis on verses 20 and 21. In this scripture, please note that when the Lord says, "they shall be thine" He is speaking to/of Aaron and the priests.

But the firstling of a cow, or the firstling of a sheep, or the firstling of a goat, thou shalt not redeem; they are holy: thou shalt sprinkle their blood upon the altar, and shalt burn their fat for an offering made by fire, for a sweet savour unto the Lord. And the flesh of them shall be thine, as the wave breast and as the right shoulder are thine. All the heave offerings of the holy things, which the children of Israel offer unto the Lord, have I given thee, and thy sons and thy daughters with thee, by a statute forever: it is a covenant of salt for ever before the Lord unto thee and to thy seed with thee. And the Lord spake unto Aaron, Thou shalt have no inheritance in their land, neither shalt thou have any part among them: I am thy part and thine inheritance among the children of Israel. And, behold, I have given the children of Levi all the tenth in Israel for an inheritance, for their service which they serve, even the service of the tabernacle of the congregation. Numbers 18:16-21

Verses 20 and 21 go to emphasize why in the entire scripture the tithe was NEVER in monetary terms. Even when you sold your harvest, God insisted that when you get to where you need to pay your tithe, convert the money back to food, gather the widows and others and then feast on the tithe. So, you will see on careful study of scriptures that, the tithe was a system of provision set up by God mainly to feed the priests and the less priviledged and it was mandated to be food ONLY.

Thou shalt truly tithe all the increase of thy seed, that the field bringeth forth year by year. And thou shalt eat before the Lord thy God, in the place which he shall choose to place his name there, the tithe of thy corn, of thy wine, and of thine oil, and the firstlings of thy herds and of thy flocks; that thou mayest learn to fear the Lord thy God always. And if the way be too long for thee, so that thou art not able to carry it; or if the place be too far from thee, which the Lord thy God shall choose to set his name there, when the Lord thy God hath blessed thee: Then shalt thou turn it into money, and bind up the money in thine hand, and shalt go unto the place which the Lord thy God shall choose: And thou shalt bestow that money for whatsoever thy soul lusteth after, for oxen, or for sheep, or for wine, or for strong drink, or for whatsoever thy soul desireth: and thou shalt eat there before the Lord thy God, and thou shalt rejoice, thou, and thine household, And the Levite that is within thy gates; thou shalt not forsake him; for he hath no part nor inheritance with thee. At the end of three years thou shalt bring forth all the tithe of thine increase the same year, and shalt lay it up within thy gates: And the Levite, (because he hath no part nor inheritance with thee,) and the stranger, and the fatherless, and the widow, which are within thy gates, shall come, and shall eat and be satisfied; that the Lord thy God may bless thee in all the work of thine hand which thou doest. Deuteronomy 14:22-29.

Notice that in this scripture, it clearly says you can eat your tithe. You are to eat it with strangers, widows, and the fatherless. This is scripture and it is not me that wrote it. This tells us that the bible provides for other end points for your tithe other than the tabernacle. Also, we see again that if on the day you want to pay your tithe, you see that the place chosen for you to submit it is far, you can sell the food with you and turn it to money. However, when you get to the place, you must change again to food, so you can eat with the priests and others already mentioned. Someone might argue that it is because the Israelites were farmers and shepherds hence the emphasis on food. Two things are wrong with this argument. One is the fact that we see from the scripture above that they could sell what they have and get money, but God OBVIOUSLY did not want money as tithes. Secondly, God's Word clearly says, "That there might be meat in my house" not that there might be money in my house. Do we think God does not know the difference between food and money? God does not try to con, deceive or appear ambiguous. He says what He means and means what He says! He said, that there might be meat in my house and not money!

If we choose to go further, we will not have enough space. I encourage you to take time to study on tithing and the conclusions you arrive at will amaze you. Tithing is elementary giving for the believer. When we read Acts 4, we see that the believers did not need to speak about tithing because they gave ALL. Tithing (giving ten percent) is meant to be a school to lead the believer into deeper consecration and stewardship with God; where the believer knows God owns the hundred percent and can demand it at any time. Instead of us leading people to this place of consecration, we are emphasizing ten percent. The result? Shallow and money conscious believers. The Apostles who walked with Christ did not need to emphasize tithing because when one truly falls in love with Jesus, no amount of money is difficult to give including one hundred percent!

Beloved, you must realize that part of the problem with Christianity today is *religion and her associated practices*. The early church showed us a pattern with associated apostolic results. The day we began to suggest that they missed something, and we had the Logos to correct it was the day we introduced error and corrupted God's church. Am I against giving in church? No... absolutely not! But the new testament way of giving is not graded in percentages. God owns all of me and all I have. I give whatsoever I give to God based on that understanding. I can give 100%, 90% or even 10%. The old order of the Levitical priesthood is done away with and Jesus is my High Priest. Not the Head/Senior Pastor, General Overseer, Bishop, Apostle or Reverend but Jesus! He doesn't need the breast of a lamb, firstling of a cow, or the firstling of a sheep, or the firstling of a goat because He does not eat food. He needs first that I be engrafted into the body, worship Him in Spirit and truth and then out of this flows my giving. Does it not bother you that in the entire teachings of Christ and the apostles, not once did a pattern for tithing get mentioned. That order has been done away with in Christ. Paul mentioned that when we give, our offerings must be out of love and not compulsion... and if I may add... not compulsion of percentages or the fear of being a thief.

Every man according as he purposeth in his heart, so let him give; not grudgingly, or of necessity: for God loveth a cheerful giver. 2 Corinthians 9:7

People might say but Abraham tithed even before the law. So, if you say the priesthood has been abolished, Abraham did not tithe under the Aaronic priesthood. I agree but notice that this that Abraham did was a ONE-OFF tithe such that scriptures mention his son Levi who was yet unborn is considered to have given tithes in Abraham. Nowhere in scriptures do you see it mentioned that Abraham tithed before or after this meeting with Melchisedec. Nowhere is it mentioned that Abraham tithes monthly either. I will like to posit that this must have been a personal revelation to Abraham and not a pattern instituted by God for all men to follow. Read all of Hebrew 7 to get a thorough understanding of this discuss. Space and time will not permit me to go further.

Do you tithe 10% in your local church? Are you doing it out of love for Jesus or because you don't want to be a thief or go to hell? Is it something you are doing by personal revelation? These are the issues not what a preacher says. I have always tithed. Some period in my life I even went above the normal 10%. Till today, my giving exceeds ten percent. But the question is, what drives my tithing and giving? Religion always emphasizes actions and doing but with authentic Christianity and before the Father-God, it is motives that count. You don't need to feel guilty if you give genuinely to God and yet do not "tithe" (give ten percent). What is ten percent, when you give to Kingdom work and advancement much more on a monthly basis? That voice screaming in your heart is the voice of condemnation trying to enforce religion and not the voice of God. Unless the Lord has specifically spoken to you on an order to follow in your giving, the standard for the new testament church is clear; give out of love and not by compulsion. Ten percent is a good place to start especially for those people who have not learnt how to give to God, His people and for His work. For some, if the tithe did not exist, they will never give to God. So, the tithe then becomes a "school" to teach you sacrifice and commitment. Otherwise, under the new covenant, the emphasis is not on percentage but on the principle of giving our ALL to Jesus.

In modern day Christianity, in the name of honour we have erroneously or inadvertently exalted the words of men above the Words of God. Men have been raised to such dizzying heights so much so that when they venture into error or apostasy we are unable to discern. Younger preachers are counselled to give "honour" to "spiritual uplines" so as to make progress in ministry. I have no problem with honouring the grace of God upon men whom God has sent ahead of us. What bothers me is, where is the pattern in scripture? On what basis have we developed prophet offerings? Where was it recorded that Elisha gave Elijah anything apart from service? Where in the relationship between Paul and Timothy or Paul and Titus did we find such relationship founded on giving properties or money to "spiritual uplines"? Now, we have forms people need to fill where they indicate as part of the covenant relationship, a vow to pay their tithes to the "spiritual upline". *Religion* is damaging my generation and my heart bleeds!

I was in a meeting once where a man was being exalted to a higher office. And when the senior pastor was speaking on this man's behavior he mentioned that this was a man who had never disobeyed authority; whatever he was told to do, that was what he did. I sat there wondering if all that is necessary for a man to hold such a high office was just loyalty to the denomination and church structure. What happened to a genuine encounter with God? What happened to actually seeking and confirming God's will for the vacant position? What happened to the fruit and gift of the Holy Spirit? I tell you what… *RELIGION* happened! So, men in structured or organized denominations in order to get promoted engage in ministry politics and all kinds of eye-service just to curry favour or please certain leaders. Beloved, please note that ministry is a spiritual assignment. There are pathways in the Spirit to fulfilling God's agenda. In the things of the Spirit, man cannot promote you it is only God. Being exalted to a higher office in your denomination doesn't necessarily mean you have been promoted by God in ministry. In the eyes of God promotion comes when you have downloaded new mysteries from the scrolls He has prepared for your assignment. If there is nothing fresh upon your spirit and man has given you a new title, all you have is a title with no mantle from Yahweh. A new title does not necessarily guarantee the supply of His Spirit upon a man. Hence, the proliferation of men in high places with no true spiritual results or impact in our generation. The Apostles of old showed us the pattern *"For we cannot but speak the things which we have seen and heard"* Act 4:20. It is what you have seen and heard from the celestial realm that authorizes you to speak on behalf of God in this terrestrial realm. If you have seen and heard nothing yet hold a towering title, you are fake and an impostor; promoted and celebrated by men but relegated and unapproved by God.

Whether intended or not, that senior pastor had sent a message to all who were seated in the meeting that day, that loyalty was more important than true spirituality.

We have created a protocol in Christendom that shuts your mouth. Why should you be challenging the status quo? People are told not to ask questions; so, frustrations continue to build. We all know these things are not working but we all continue just for the sake of it. After all, we all met it this way. It has always been like this and we are not the ones to now come and change it. People are offended when one attempts to challenge the status quo. Like a Pastor said, "if you are offended that we are challenging the status quo, then something is wrong with you".

Everything we enjoy in Christendom today are products of men like Martin Luther, John Wycliffe, John Wesley and so many others challenging the status quo. These men confronted the religious establishment of their day and gave us the protestant reformation, the bible in English and deeper experiences with God even at the expense of their own lives. I can tell you dear believer that strange men are rising again. A new stream is being furnished in the realms and genuine apostolic Christianity is on the rise. The end of the pulpit ministry as we know it is here; "unknown" men and women without titles shall again take nations for Jesus. I hear this clearly in my spirit.

We cannot be pursuing our Christian walk "just for the sake of it" There has got to be more than we are experiencing now. You cannot continue to pretend that all those questions raging in your heart have been answered because it will rob you of a genuine experience with God. It is time we demand answers... enough of *religion and religious activity*. We want authentic Christianity.

Oh God! Where is our evidence? Where is the evidence that we have been with Christ? I wish you will ponder on this as you read this book. If indeed we say God lives in us, where is the evidence?

If indeed you are a believer, why is your life not producing the results Jesus shows us are possible in scripture? *"And these signs will accompany those who believe: In my name they will drive out demons; they will speak in new tongues; they will pick up snakes with their hands; and when they drink deadly poison, it will not hurt them at all; they will place their hands on sick people, and they will get well."* Mark 16:16-18. If you have indeed believed and call yourself a believer, where are the results as spelt out by Jesus in this scripture?

Why are you not enjoying the manifest presence of the Holy Spirit like those who walked the earth before us? Why are you praying, fasting and doing all you can and yet there are no changes in your life? We cannot continue doing the same things and expect different results. It is time to confront these anomalies and produce results. I can assure you the limit is never on God's end of the equation.

Acts 4: 13-14
"Now when they saw the boldness of Peter and John, and perceived that they were unlearned and ignorant men, they marveled; and they took knowledge of them that they had been with Jesus. And beholding the man which was healed standing with them, they could say nothing against it" KJV

Let us see this same verse in another translation:
"Now when they saw the boldness and unfettered eloquence of Peter and John and perceived that they were unlearned and untrained in the schools [common men with no educational advantages], they marveled; and they recognized that they had been with Jesus. And since they saw the man who had been cured standing there beside them, they could not contradict the fact or say anything in opposition." AMP

The Sanhedrin; rulers, scribes and priests wanted to shut Peter and John up but proof that they had been with Jesus was too powerful to ignore. The amplified translation as shown above says "they could not contradict the fact or say anything in opposition". This had nothing to do with where they fellowshipped or who their General Overseer was. This was a simple result of a personal encounter. The men of the Sanhedrin recognized that these ordinary men; common men with no educational advantage were producing extraordinary results because of one thing and one thing only. They had been with Jesus.

Can we in our generation imagine this same result in our time? How many Christians can truly provide proofs of their encounter with Jesus? Can we "shut up" atheists, juju priests and jihadists in our community with our results? I leave that for you to ponder on. These are the sort of questions that ravage my heart and push me to my knees.

Religious people wanted to shut them up but right there standing beside them was the man who everyone knew used to be lame in both feet. *Religion wanted to enforce the protocol of silence* but when they heard these ignorant and unlearned men speak, men who had never been to school and who had no degree in theology nor any educational advantages, the religious people marveled for they knew, only a genuine encounter with divinity can produce such results. They concluded without being cajoled or forced; indeed, these men have been with Jesus.

Ah! My heart bleeds! *Enough of religion and religious activity*. We must resist it with all that we have. Enough of men gathering us in buildings yet our lives cannot seem to produce proofs of a genuine encounter. Enough of men emphasizing giving of tithes, offerings and special seeds yet our secret lives are covered in the stench of easy besetting sins. Enough of men emphasizing public service and commitment to church doctrines yet our personal lives lack consecration, discipline and genuine worship of the Father-God. We must look ourselves in the mirror and tell the person who we see therein "If I have no proofs then probably what I have been calling an encounter with God has been nothing but *religious activity*". Every encounter with Jesus produces men who can add value to the world.

We seem to have more educational advantages than the saints of old. We have Doctors of Divinity, Doctors of Theology, Professors of one field or the other, skilled and eloquent preachers, masters of the exegesis of scripture and great teachers of the Word. Yet we have so little results. What did the saints of old have or know that despite their little education they still had tremendous power with God and over men? It is our responsibility to study their lives and ensure we too gain the advantage that is greater than educational advantages. I hope to deal with this in another chapter of this book.

I ask you again; if you are indeed a believer, where is your evidence? Have you been with Jesus? If you have, where are your proofs?

I sincerely pray that your picking this book to read will begin a journey towards true impactful Christian living in your life. I am believing that the heavens will open over you and God will speak directly to your heart. My earnest desire is that there be a stirring in your heart for genuine spiritual progress and your engaging this book brings you face to face with the only true God Yahweh.

I pray also that you read this with an open heart; sometimes your head will wonder "what is he saying here?" but I assure you, your heart will know I speak the truth. I encourage you to listen to the voice of the Spirit as He engages your heart.

If we do not change our ways and return again to the ancient paths, we would raise a generation that knows not God and all we would have to show for the life of Christ in us will be large auditoriums and gatherings without the life-giving Spirit of God. We will raise a generation of ministers whose passion in ministry will be prosperity and material wealth… But I assure you, this is not the proof of the gospel. The proof of the gospel is in the evidence of changed lives, the outflow of God's power, the manifestation of the convicting presence of God on our streets, in our communities, cities and countries and the return of genuine revival across our lands.

Religion must have no place in our lives. Our pastors must go back to teaching the true Word of God as it should be taught;

with simplicity and genuineness. We must create an appetite in the lives of our church members for the kind of experiences the men who have lived before us had. Except we do this, we would continue in this cycle and how sad it would be for us all.

With this book and God's intervention, may religion have its last word in our lives and may we cry with hunger for God and all that He truly represents.

I encourage you at this moment to stop, meditate and pray as led by the Holy Spirit. Press into the realms, seek an audience with the Great One, cry for a fresh outpouring and do not get up from your knees until something genuine happens to you. Let your heart rise in yearnings that words cannot give form until your spirit utters groanings that mortal man cannot understand.

There is a place beloved, a place where God is real, and His presence can be felt. But there is way; Jesus points us to the way as Job put it *"There is a path which no fowl knoweth, and which the vulture's eye hath not seen: The lion's whelps have not trodden it, nor the fierce lion passed by it"* Job 28:7-8.

Pray for yourself, this writer and the entire body of Christ. We must not allow *religion* thrive in our midst. We desire the manifestation of authentic Christianity. We want the knowledge of His glory to cover the earth....

Authentic Christianity is to live as Christ lived, teach what He taught and produce the same results He produced when He walked the face of the earth as God's man who was also the Son of God.

Thus saith the Lord, Stand ye in the ways, and see, and ask for the old paths, where is the good way, and walk therein, and ye shall find rest for your souls. But they said, We will not walk therein. Also I set watchmen over you, saying, Hearken to the sound of the trumpet. But they said, We will not hearken. Jeremiah 6:16-17

Let us pray...

FORM BUT NO POWER

There is nothing like comfortable Christianity.
You are what you tolerate.
– Rev. Samuel Rodriguez

And my speech and my preaching was not with enticing
words of man's wisdom, but in demonstration of
the Spirit and power:
That your faith should not stand in the
wisdom of men, but in the power of God
1 Corinthians 2:4-5

For the kingdom of God is not in word only but in the
demonstration of power
- 1 Corinthians 4:20

"The earnest (heartfelt, continued) prayer of a righteous man
makes tremendous power available (dynamic in its working)."
- James 5:16b

And with great power gave the apostles witness
of the resurrection of the Lord Jesus:
and great grace was upon them all - Acts 4:33

The gospel of Christ is the power of God unto salvation.
The gospel does not carry power the gospel is power! If the "gospel"
being preached does not produce power,
then there is something wrong with the "gospel"
and we must change it.
– Rev Williams Ogoigbe

I sat in one of our Christian gatherings not too long ago and as I watched the number of people trooping in (in their thousands), deep down in the crevices of my soul I felt a certain sadness; I was grieving! How can we have so many people in the family of God and yet be producing so little impact in our world. It is the same in every continent of the world; we continue to have large gatherings of Christians but there seems to be a disconnect between what happens in our sanctuaries on Sundays and the lives lived on a daily basis. People jump, roll on the floor, speak in tongues, rock in their chairs but have no influence whatsoever in their families or on the people they meet at work. We profess one thing and yet live another! We say the God who lives in us is powerful and yet we cannot touch the world with His hand. There I sat and as tears welled up in my eyes, the grief seemed to increase as it dawned on me that what is most fearful in all of this is that we have somehow become comfortable with this anomaly.

What could have brought the Church to this place? Why are there so many believers yet we are not having the same kind of results like the saints who walked the earth before us. We seem to be preaching the same gospel but we wonder at the disparity in the outcomes. What the saints preached produced Christ-like believers with outstanding results. What we preach seems to be producing the opposite.

In Acts 8, the writer somehow "squeezes" in the story of Philip the Deacon somewhere around verse 5 and I couldn't help but ask what happened to this "common man" that set him on fire! His story is almost fairytale like; one day he was nobody sitting in the corner of the room, the next day he was ordained a Deacon and soon after he was working miracles and moving from place to place on the wings of the Holy Spirit. Wow! From disciple to miracle worker and eventually world changer. How did this happen?

Acts 6:1-6 tells us Deacons were chosen to serve tables. Let us make that very simple to understand; they were chosen to serve food to those who needed to eat. So, their job description was simple: when food has been cooked and meal prepared for all the disciples, the food is brought to the Deacons who then will ensure everyone present (and maybe absent) is served. This was the expectation (and obligation) on the lives of these men by the church leadership. However, the qualification was that they must be FULL of the Holy Spirit and wisdom. The Holy Spirit is power upon and power within; what that means is He works within us to produce godly character and He rests upon us so we might express the nature of God through signs and wonders in the lives of men; we can say He is in me for me and upon me to impact the world.

Philip and ALL the other Deacons were full of the Holy Spirit. How then does one need to be endued with power from on high just to serve tables? It tells me then that the gathering of the saints of old was not to glory in numbers, excite themselves and talk about denominations but to empower and release people to influence their world. When anyone came into their midst they received the Holy Spirit, became empowered and were released to do likewise to the next person they met. Proof of this was the evidence of changed attitudes and speech, love for others and the willingness to serve plus the desire and ability to change the world around you; turn the world the right side up for Jesus Christ.

"But when they failed to find them, they dragged Jason and some of the brethren before the city authorities, crying, these men who have turned the world upside down have come here also" Act 17:6 AMP

Imagine the testimony of the believers that lived before us. Wherever they went, they turned it upside down with proofs. The whole world was their stage and the audience (the people) recognized these actors as world changers. What does the world recognize us as in this generation? In most places, we are only known as noise makers because we have the multitude of words but no results. In some places, we are described as collection points for money. How sad!

The church gathering in the time of these great men was a platform for everyone to encounter God so they could go out and encounter men for God; bring men to the place where they too desired a personal deep, rich and sweet experience with God. Philip is a clear example. He was ordained to serve tables, there is no record that he was sent specifically to Samaria for a crusade, yet he walked into Samaria and affected their world. If you read Acts 8 very well you would see that it begins by telling us there was great persecution against the church and this resulted in the brethren scattering throughout the regions of Judea and Samaria. What intrigues me the most is that scriptures clearly state that only the Apostles remained in Jerusalem. It was not a scattering led by the Apostles, everyone found himself or herself alone (or probably in small groups) without the leaders of the church being with them. It is in the midst of this unusual circumstance that the writer of Acts reports the story of Philip. A man chosen to serve tables goes down to Samaria and starts a revival. A revival so powerful that even the most powerful man in the city submitted to the power of God at work in this "common man".

"But there was a certain man called Simon, which before-time in the same city used sorcery and bewitched the people of Samaria, giving out that himself was some great one: to whom they all gave heed, from the least to the greatest, saying, this man is the great power of God. And to him they had great regard, because that of long time he had bewitched them with sorceries. But when they believed Philip preaching the things concerning the kingdom of God and the name of Jesus Christ, they were baptized both men and women. Then Simon himself believed also: and when he was baptized, he continued with Philip and wondered beholding the miracles and signs which were done" Acts 8:9-13.

The bible records that the entire city was full of GREAT joy (Acts 8:8). Thus, Philip did not need the Apostles to be present to walk in the same dimension they obviously had been operating in. He obviously had been taught that the same Holy Spirit they had received lived in him and he too could walk in the same dimensions as made available by the power within and upon him. News began to spread everywhere that Philip had turned Samaria right-side-up; the story filtered into the ears of the church leaders (Apostles) in Jerusalem and they sent Peter and John to take over; they came laid hands on the new converts and these new converts received the Holy Spirit. See Acts 8:14-17. Stop!

Imagine this scenario in our modern day organized religion especially in Nigeria. Our denomination leaders would have first sent a team of "deliverance ministers" who when they had gotten the news of what Philip had done in Samaria, would have started a 21 day fast to prepare for the task ahead. On arrival, they would have crammed all the people together in some room somewhere and started some form of indoctrination to damage the simple experience these new converts had. I can imagine them saying "Since you have been under this great man Simon who has been bewitching you, demons from your father's house and witches from your mother's house have taken over your destiny. Before you can move on, you must be delivered" Then they would throw in Obadiah 1:17 for good measure "Upon mount Zion there will be deliverance and holiness and then the house of Jacob will possess their possession." So, before you can possess your possession you must be delivered! And these saints whom God just saved will now be fed erroneous teaching that corrupts the simplicity of the gospel which brought about their deliverance.

Beloved, believing in Jesus and confessing with your mouth that He is Lord of your life is deliverance in itself. The pattern is clearly shown by the Apostles; after the acceptance of Jesus into their hearts, then the convert receives the Holy Spirit. Why is this important? I cannot be full of God and full of demons at the same time it is just not possible. So, to say a believer is possessed is wrong teaching! You find someone who says "I have the Holy Spirit but my Pastor says I need deliverance" The question then is, deliverance from what? The word translated "Salvation" in scriptures also means to be healed and delivered! If you then need another deliverance we seem to be saying that accepting, believing, and confessing Jesus is no longer potent enough to save and we need something a little more complex to make it "powerful". This is part of my pain with organized religion. We seem to be saying to those who sit in our pews every Sunday that, "if it is not difficult, complex and painful, it is not spiritual, and it definitely cannot be God" The Bible shows that Jesus' mandate was to PREACH deliverance to the captives. Notice the word used "Preach". He cast out devils from them who were unbelievers, but He preached deliverance to the captives. Captives as used in this verse speak of those who have been brought under the yoke of Christ. They have been captured by Jesus and become yoked with Him. To them He preached deliverance to bring them into a consciousness of their position in God. See Luke 4:18.

A Pastor shared that if it were to be our generation of believers that arrived at the red sea, we would start a prayer meeting to "shout" and call upon God to intervene while we set-up a church committee to raise funds to build a bridge across the sea. I believe what this Pastor was trying to show is what our state in this generation is; our outlook in the circumstance will seem to be one of faith but our actions will betray the true conditions of our heart.

Honestly beloved, the story of Philip in Acts 8 humbles and at the same time challenges me. The simplicity of it all makes what we do in present day look so ominous.

I can imagine; after the Apostles laid hands and the converts received the Holy Spirit, they would have heard a simple message like "Now you too are born-again! You have accepted Jesus and received the promised Holy Spirit. Go now and preach the kingdom of God. What you saw Philip do, you too can now do. Go now!" End of story! Not a list of how many were saved or how we need to start a church here or how they need to come and be reporting to the Apostles every day or whatever thing we have come up with in our present day organized religion that we now call Christianity. Is it any surprise then, that when compared to the simplicity of the saints before us we seem to have better methods but pale in comparism to their results? We have methods they had men!

Like that was not enough, God asks Philip to wait by the roadside for another assignment. What humbles me here is, when Philip was done opening scriptures to the Ethiopian eunuch, he baptizes the man and when they came up out of the water, the Spirit of the Lord took Philip away on His wings to another city called Azotus. In fact, scriptures record that "Philip was found at Azotus: and passing through he preached in all the cities till he came to Caesarea" Acts 8:26-40

Every time I read these stories about Philip I am undone (Like the prophet said in Isaiah 6:5) because I only wonder what he could have been hearing from the lips of the Apostles that gave him the confidence to go out and produce God-like results. Even Apostle Peter who was considered the leader of the team did not experience the chariot of the Holy Spirit like Philip did. What then happened inside of Philip that caused him to step out in faith? I dare say it was the gospel that was being preached to him daily and the personal encounters he pursued with God as a result of the gospel being preached.

If the church in present day will change this ominous trajectory, we must stop leading men into traditions and religion but into encounters with the Most High. A genuine personal encounter with God provides more education on the spiritual life than millions of years of theological teaching.

A man called to serve tables did not need taxis or cabs he moved on the wagon of the Holy Spirit. I wonder if those who clean our church sanctuaries or those who stand at the gates as security guards/officers can operate at this same level in our modern-day Christianity. Of course not! Because there seems to be a silent agreement that we need to gather somewhere, under someone for this kind of experience to happen. No sir! We need to start telling people the truth about the gospel. Christ came to restore us to the family of God so we too could begin to walk in the same power that Christ walked in while on earth.

We have Christians who hang on every word spoken by their general overseers, bishops, prophets, primates, evangelists, apostles and so on but they cannot even believe the written Word of God. They do not know anything about the bible and God's promises to us as believers all they know is what their bishop or pastor said to them. Organized religion has helped us grow believers who will defend the words of their pastors with the last drop of their blood but cannot defend the Word of God in their hearts when they face trials, temptations and spiritual attacks. We have become a frozen set of people; the cold is not without but within; our hearts are cold; frozen cold by the words of men for if it were the Word of God that had captured our hearts we would like Jeremiah say, *"Your Word is as a burning fire shut-up in my bones". Jeremiah 20:9.*

What has brought the Church to this point? Religion! Organized Religion!!

We think what we have is Christianity, but I tell you it is organized religion. Where we are spreading all over the world; various church names, different denominations, well dressed preachers and fat bank accounts but no evidence of changed lives. We cannot readily differentiate between us and the world system anymore. We have taken what the world has to offer laced it with some tongues and grafted it into our lives. Religion has become a stronghold and little wonder we are a powerless generation. We have form; we look like the saints of old, but we do not hunger for the same rich inner experiences that can produce wonderful outer manifestations. So, the church has become a laughing stock we say one thing and our lives produce another. What we celebrate as results, you do not necessarily need to be a Christian to enjoy them. In fact, people have begun to ask "where is their God?" In Nigeria, you only need to walk a few feet from your house to hear a church praying (on top of their voices); some killing enemies, others crying to God for deliverance, while the rest "are just praying". Yet we walk out of those prayer meetings, church services, vigils and still have no "meaningful" impact on our world. Where are Christians in politics? Where are Christians taking the lead in medicine? Where are Christians shining the light of God in business? We are constantly at the back of the line, yet we are always screaming on top of our voices in so called church buildings! I can imagine those who walk pass asking, "Where is their God?" If He is as powerful as they infer He is when they pray, how come that man (probably pointing at someone in the congregation) cannot even influence his neighbourhood?"

Beloved of God, as a man of God mentioned, "The world is not waiting for a NEW DEFINITION of the gospel but a NEW DEMONSTRATION of the power of the gospel". The world has heard us pray all night, shout on the top of our voices but their eyes have never really seen, and their souls never felt the power of divine visitation. We have form but there is no power! If by praying prayers against enemies and village curses alone nations have become great, then Nigeria should have been the greatest nation on earth. If by gathering in huge numbers in church buildings (some too small to hold all of us) peoples and communities have been changed, then Nigeria should have become the most transformed nation on the planet! If by the number of churches in the land alone economies have been transformed, then Nigeria would indeed have been a great economy. Yet we are poor, sick, hungry, suffering, underdeveloped and considered a third world country. What worries me is that despite all of these, Christians are even the more so comfortable! These are things we are told not to talk about. When one dares mention them, you are told you need to mature and grow up. We have developed doctrines around faith so that when we cannot produce the results the people demand, we say they don't have enough faith. We are representatives of a superior King and kingdom, yet we cannot exert His influence in this world. I fear that very soon real-life situations will arise to challenge the professions we are making and not many in this generation will be able to stand to defend the faith. Some of us are indeed professing Christians but we have nothing but religious activity to support our professions. What worries and saddens me is that we are very comfortable... No one seems to be challenging the status quo.

Religion tells us to continue searching for better methods (larger billboards, "7 step recipes", ICT/Tech Savvy churches, financial teaching and sowing of seeds etc.) while God continues to say "I search for better men". Men who are not satisfied with the comfort of our so-called church buildings but see the sanctuary as an incubator to hatch men of faith and substance who can influence their world. Men who are given to prayer not for enemies, food for the belly or clothes for their backs but that the Kingdom of God be established on earth. Men of the secret place; who have given themselves to genuine agonizing prayer for the latter-day church. The bible says the glory of the latter house shall be greater than that of the former. Sadly, it seems we are back to asking, "who saw this house in its former glory?" because what should be greater is nowhere near the expectations we have of it. We seem to be celebrating mediocrity while God is lamenting for His church.

The death of Christ was to bring us victory over the enemy and empower us to bring the influence of God's kingdom upon the earth, but we seem to be holding ourselves back as slaves to religion and religious activity. Our enemy was dealt with on the cross our job is to walk in the consciousness of the victory Christ wrought on Calvary. Anything less is not correct!

I am worried brethren that very soon Church will only be a place where we come to feel "safe" while the whole world around us crumbles. It seems to me that we are going back into Noah's ark only that this time God is not purging the world of sin, but God's man is refusing to reach the world with God's love and power. We hide in the comfort of our sanctuary buildings, seemingly affirm that our God has power to do the impossible, but when we step into the world no one notices that we have been with God. Peter at the fire warming his hands and trying so much to hide who he truly was, was jolted back to life with the cry from the lips of a little girl "You are one of His disciples, your speech betrays you". Oh, how I wish when we step out of our church buildings, men strung together and bound by the evil systems of the world would point fingers at us and say "the nature and glory of God upon you betrays you. Indeed, you are a child of God". The truth is, as Jesus speaking said "YE ARE THE LIGHT OF THE WORLD AND THE SALT OF THE EARTH" (Mathew 5:13-16) and added in Mathew 17:20 "if ye believe... nothing shall be impossible unto you", there is a demand for us to standout in the fullness of God's power and glory. I do not know how anyone can read these two portions of scripture penned as the spoken Word of Christ Himself and not be ashamed at our lack of desire to see this manifest in this generation. I weep, oh I weep! Day and night, I cry in the secret place of my bedroom; my heart grieves, for religion has enslaved us and kept us content with mediocre Christianity. Did He not say, ye are gods? How come we have no impact whatsoever over nations, economies, diseases and sicknesses?

Just recently in Nigeria and indeed some parts of Africa we experienced an outbreak of Ebola disease. Governments were at their wits end on how to tackle the scourge, people were dying and, yet the church could not offer a simple solution. Not one preacher dared to publicly command the scourge to seize. We were all in our buildings praying yet on the outside people were dying. As each day breaks and ends, on our Christian television stations we see healing evangelists "brandishing their wares" trying to outdo one another but no one could dare rise and tackle this menace. If for any reason the epidemic spread in Nigeria, people would just have been dying like flies and we would have been in our buildings "praying". Imagine this same scenario in the time of Paul, Peter or Philip or even evangelists and preachers of old. What exactly do you think would have happened? Several years ago, a plague broke out somewhere in Africa. The slightest contact with any secretion from an infected person is all it took for transmission. But with his bare hands; cleaning secretion, helping victims and carrying the dead, John G Lake supported the medical crew who were clothed head to toe in body suits. When confronted, he asked them to get a sample from an infected person, observe same under a microscope to ascertain viral activities in it. They did and confirmed living and multiplying virus. He then asked them to put the sample on his palm and observe under the microscope. When they checked, they found that the virus on contact with John G. Lakes' palm died instantly. When he was asked the secret, he said "great is the mystery of godliness. I have the life of Christ in me". Oh Lord!

What influence then does the church have over the world? Have we become so irrelevant that kings no longer come to the brightness of our rising? I challenge every believer to go read scriptures. You will discover that men like Peter, Paul, John the Baptist, and our saviour Jesus Christ all had tremendous influence over the nations where they found themselves. A man of God in Nigeria while speaking concerning the Ebola situation said "not even one man of God in Nigeria could send a handkerchief to the government to help stop the plague. Why? Because anyone who attempted it, it would amount putting his/her entire reputation at stake" I don't think there are men who would dare do that now. Not in my generation. Think about it, I hope I am wrong.

We have preachers who do not even believe in what they preach. If they do, it would reflect in their actions daily. For instance, we say God can provide yet we go to take loans to build our churches. If indeed it is God's project, He would finance it. Without us having to fleece, cajole or manipulate our church workers or members.

All we are concerned about is growing large churches, building exquisite state of the art facilities, gathering more money in the name of doing God's work and making a name for ourselves. While the world around us perishes. Hence some Pastors have become more popular than Jesus; the messenger has become more important than the message he carries. How dreadful!

Jesus was very clear in this regard. In Mathew 5:13 *He said "ye are the salt of the earth: but if the salt have lost his savour wherewith shall it be salted? It is thenceforth good for nothing, but to be cast out, and to be trodden under foot"* Simply put, a purposeless life is a useless life. The church seems to have forgotten her purpose. We seem to be focusing our energies in the wrong places and on the wrong things. We are no longer raising men who God can use but growing large denominations so we have form and no power. Invariably we have lost our savour. What then are we good for? As Jesus said, nothing! Are we now surprised that the world no longer takes us seriously?

How did we become so satisfied with mediocrity in Christendom? How did we become so comfortable with the "abnormal"? How did we get to this point where we can no longer manifest God everywhere we go? I tell you how; the leaders who should have preached the correct gospel have not told us the whole truth. We must admit that for some they didn't know better but for most, their personal validation in life and ministry comes from seeing the church pews full and they are constantly doing everything to keep everybody coming back. The priority has shifted; we now want bigger sanctuary buildings, larger crowds, acceptance from the world and are now trapped in the devil's game of numbers. If we are bigger then we must be succeeding. So, we have form but no power, trees but no depth, and Christians with no personal encounters or experiences with God; the Pastor's personal experience is enough for all of us! So, people are "discouraged" from seeking God for themselves; all you need do is come to the Pastor, Bishop or General Overseer and all will be well! No Sir! All is not well! We have millions of people in sanctuaries but we have just a handful who know why they really gather. Others just come to hear the preacher or enjoy the "entertainment" that has been put up for them by their various denominations.

Invariably we now have a gospel that teaches "giving" but does not tell the people that giving alone would not get you to prosper. People are giving all they have in the name of giving to God, but they are dying in poverty and want. We cannot then reconcile the leaders in the pulpit (the lavish way they dress, the sumptuous meals they eat, the luxurious cars they drive and houses they live in) with the peasants in the pew who come every Sunday to "give to God" in the sanctuary. God said our tithes and offerings are given so that they would be meat in His house. Yes, the priest was to take his portion but everyone (one way or the other; directly or indirectly) was also supposed to benefit from the gift brought to God's house. This is why the Apostles after Jesus had gone, they did everything in common i.e. no one said this is mine or that is yours, but everything was brought to the Apostles feet and distributions were made to those that had needs. But religion tells you that is outdated Christianity. Now we build schools with seeds, offerings and tithes of the church members yet their children cannot attend these schools. I humbly ask the sincere leader to provide me an answer; what would the saints of old have done in this situation? Would they have had schools that other Christians cannot attend, or would they have made sure they had the best structures, equipment and curriculum and yet ensured every believer could access it? I leave us to our consciences!

Enough of gathering in meetings and yet having no influence on our world! Enough of chasing demons, devils and village enemies. Enough of false doctrines and erroneous teachings. It is time to fall on our knees and cry unto God until we be covered with power from on high; until we can change the course of

Nations and the world around us. Scriptures say, *"nothing shall be impossible unto you"* Mathew 17:20. Enough of blaming witchcraft for our woes; it is time to take our place as sons and daughters. Where is our God? The God I know is more than able; there is no lack of ability or limitation with Jehovah! That the knowledge of His glory will cover the earth like the waters cover the sea.

A wise man once said "With all thy getting, get unction!" Don't allow yourself become "one of those Christians" but by any means necessary, determine to influence your world during and after your lifetime. Some people's influence even though they are dead and buried are larger than some of us who are alive... yet we all received the same Holy Ghost!

The secret is an insatiable hunger for a genuine encounter with God. I am yet to meet a man that encountered God and became satisfied. The more you know Him, the more you want to know Him. The more of Himself He pours into your life, the more your soul yearns for another infilling. There seems to be something about God and the believer; God continues to pursue us as we also pursue Him and yet when we apprehend Him the pursuit continues. We should be satisfied when we drink from His well, but we thirst to be thirsty still! He satisfies us that we might hunger still! This is the proof of a genuine encounter with our savior. Scriptures are replete with examples – Jesus looks at the disciples and says, "Will you also leave me?" Peter says "To whom shall we go? With You are the Words of life" see John 6:67 -68. It seems to me he is saying I have tasted and, yet I want more. Paul who wrote more than half of the New Testament; a man that received such deep revelations from God still cried out "That I may know Him…" How could he have received so much "knowing" from God and still cry for more? Something unique happened inside Paul.

If we do not kill religion and religious activity now, it will become the greatest threat to the church. Very soon real situations will arise in our nations to test our faith and the truth about our state will be glaring for all to see.

We must begin to point men to the kind of deep personal experiences with God that saints of old craved and enjoyed. The average Christian has a very shallow inner experience and is not worth his salt. Like Tozer said, "we have come in by saying "I accept Christ". We signed the card; we joined something, but we have not really met God". The Church cannot afford to continue churning this kind of Christians out of the assembly lines of our denominations. We must at this time do a right-about-face (U-turn) and show men who they have become in their contact with Christ. We must let people know that the burden of God is not just to feed, clothe, heal and prosper us but that the kingdom of heaven might have uttermost influence over the earth. Religion wants us depending on our preachers and prophets for things we can get directly from God. I wonder if there are preachers in this generation who can tell the large flocks you do not have to travel all the way from your house to attend this "special convention" if you can watch on television or tune in via the internet God can meet you where you are. Better still if you can kneel before God you have the right that I have with God and as such can get the same results. The situation where in some denominations people are afraid to miss "special programs" organized by church leadership or hierarchy because they will be punished has led to us having full auditoriums but powerless believers. The Word of God can only bring profiting when it is mixed with faith and faith comes by hearing the Word. When one has been "forced" to attend a meeting so as not to be labelled carnal or not spiritual what do you think he or she would hear throughout the meeting? This is why most people are just going through the motions. They are singing in the choir, ushering at their duty posts, filling the pews but having no impact on their world.

Dear preacher, if you are indeed preaching the gospel which is the power of God, you would know. The people who leave your sanctuary building will not be saying one thing and living another or saying one thing and producing an opposite result.

Let people serve out of love and not compulsion. When they seat in front of you on Sunday, you must ensure you have spent time with God to get a word to encourage, admonish and empower. So, when they leave they go into the world to make impact. You are not the message sir! Hear me ma, you are not the message! Point them to the risen Christ and the power of His resurrection. I fear that, so many Church leaders are in danger of hell not because they didn't preach but because consciously and unconsciously they have taken the place of God in the hearts of men. God said my name is jealous for I am a jealous God. I will not share my glory with another. When your member or church worker is now more afraid of you than God, then there is a problem!

I wish that those reading this book will do so with an open mind. I am not against us meeting in a sanctuary and fellowshipping together. Neither am I against denominations spreading all over the world. In fact, I am a firm believer in fellowship and devotion to fellowship. Bible clearly says we should not forsake the assembly of brethren – I have dealt with this in the first chapter. We should meet, pray together, encourage one another but we must ensure we are not building dependent Christians. We should not be afraid to lead from the place of servanthood. We should tell the people what our jobs really are as preachers. We are to show them who they are in Christ and not teach them to depend on us and our prayers for results. God is the one who gives results and anyone who comes to him has the same right as the preacher in the pulpit. The flock belongs to the Master. The preacher is just the shepherd reporting to the Chief Shepherd; Christ. A problem exists when the preacher defines himself and validates his call by the number of sheep under him. I tell those I am priviledged to lead – "I am just a guide".

Some of us have created meetings for everyday of the week, the so-called church workers are worn out from balancing their commitment to the denomination and their secular jobs and we hound them or make them feel like they are disobeying God because they cannot be in every meeting or gathering. Let the focus shift from trying to keep the sheep to empowering them to be who they are supposed to be in Christ. Let our prayer points change from the place of defeatism to praying from the understanding of righteousness and son-ship. Let us tell them who they are so they can go out and do like Philip did... Impact the world! If this shift will happen then power will return to the Church.

"I marvel that ye are so soon removed from him that called you into the grace of Christ unto another gospel: which is not another; but there be some that trouble you and would pervert the gospel of Christ. But though we, or an angel from heaven preach any other gospel unto you than that which we have preached unto you let him be accursed" Galatians 1:6-8

Will you be part of the revolution?
I wonder what it will be like when we begin to see empowered Christians in politics, academics, sports, medicine and even Christendom. A player slumps on the field while playing rugby and the empowered Christian does not think of calling his pastor but walks up there, lays hands and the player is revived! The widow who is a cleaner in a school, has no money to feed not to talk of paying hospital bills but has been taught that she is the righteousness of God in Christ Jesus and can stand in the presence of the Father without the sense of guilt and shame. She is called home that her only child is dying she doesn't think of running to the sanctuary building to see her pastor because her pastor has taught her that the same power that raised Christ from the dead is at work in her instead she lays her hands and the child comes alive. What a country Nigeria will be, the continents of the world will be rocking, news tabs would be full of breaking news just like it was in Jesus' day, Peter's day, Philip's day and Paul's day. Hallelujah! This is what it means to be free from the hold of organized religion.

God please bring this to pass in my day!
"The first work of the Spirit is to give life – spiritual life. He gives it and sustains it. If there is no life, there can be no power"
– D.L Moody

What Does It Mean To Work For God?

*There is probably not another field of human activity
where there is so much waste as in the field of religion.
It is altogether possible to waste an hour in
church or even in a prayer meeting.*
– *A. W Tozer*

*And whatsoever ye do, do it heartily, as to the Lord,
and not unto men;*
- *Col 3:23.*

*The scripture above doesn't mean it is God's work per se,
what it means is, I do it like I am doing it for God.
When we work in the Church we are working for the denomination
we belong and not necessarily for God.*
– *K.H. Esiri*

Now this would sound like "blasphemy" in the ears of many but I think I am willing to brave the "stones".

This "working for God" matter is one of the many abuses of the Christian faith by organized religion and I wish every believer will carefully read and appreciate what God has put in my heart to write in this chapter of the book.

I believe the challenge we have as believers is when we hear the word church we equate it with the "House of God". I have learnt differently, and this has helped shape the way I approach my work for and walk with God.

Christianity must first be a personal walk before it can become a public service. To have the latter and not the former would be pitiful. To emphasize the latter and not the former would produce religious people and not authentic Christians. This for me is the highest form of hypocrisy. Too many church people have public service without personal consecration and this has led to a somewhat fatal emphasis on externalism as against the desired focus on the flames burning in the heart as a result of a commitment to the secret place.

Let me state some truths before I deal with this.
The word translated Church in the New Testament is the Greek

word "Ekklesia" and for every time it was used in the bible, it NEVER referred to a building. Every time it was used in scriptures it referred to a gathered people and not a building. The House of God concept comes from the Old Testament where God tells Moses to build a tabernacle so He can dwell in the midst of His people. *"And let them make me a sanctuary; that I may dwell among them."* Exo 25:8 KJV

In the Old Testament, before we ever saw a building, Jacob is on the run from his brother Esau and comes to a place on his journey where he decides to rest. He takes some stones, makes a pillow, falls asleep and has a dream. In his dream, he sees a ladder connecting heaven and earth, angels ascending and descending, and God standing at the top of the ladder. God then introduces Himself as the God of his fathers - Abraham and Isaac. What intrigues me here is what Jacob says when he wakes up. *"And Jacob awaked out of his sleep, and he said, Surely the Lord is in this place; and I knew it not. And he was afraid, and said, How dreadful is this place! this is none other but the house of God, and this is the gate of heaven. And Jacob rose up early in the morning, and took the stone that he had put for his pillows, and set it up for a pillar, and poured oil upon the top of it. And he called the name of that place Bethel: but the name of that city was called Luz at the first"* Gen 28:16-19

You will notice from the portions I highlighted that, it was because of the presence of God that Jacob experienced that made him to name the place Beth (house) of El (God). Remember that this was in the middle of "no-where" without buildings so it would seem Jacob didn't know what he was saying or doing by calling an empty space a house. What God introduces to us here is that, wherever God's presence is manifest that is his house it has nothing to do with a building. If God can be present in your living room, then your house can be called Bethel. Just as it is His presence that makes our denominational buildings a church.

If we move further in the old testament, we had a moveable tent in the wilderness which if you permit me I would like to call the tabernacle of Moses; basically, because he received the specific instructions of how it should be built. This tent in certain places in scripture was also referred to as the tabernacle of meeting. The people went to the tabernacle to meet with God. However, there were different chambers in the tabernacle to define varying levels of intimacy in relationship with God. We had the outer court, the inner court and the holy of holies. Only the high priest was allowed to enter the holy of holies and commune to and with God on behalf of himself and the people. The Hebrews had an understanding that when they came into the tabernacle they had come into God's house. Now is this correct? Yes, it is!

This is how God chose to relate with His people at that time because man's sin had severed Him from God and God could not fellowship with man like He used to in the garden because sin had created a gulf. God then had to create a platform for humanity to meet divinity (howbeit temporarily) until He had dealt with the sin issue. Now to take this and continue to walk in this understanding will not be correct because things have changed.

When Christ came, John tells us the Word became flesh and dwelt amongst us. The word translated "dwelt" here also means tabernacle. So, if I were to read that again it would read something like this "the Word became flesh and tabernacled upon us". This is of immense importance because it goes back to what God has been trying to achieve since man fell in the garden; God wants intimate fellowship with man on a platform where man can stand before God guiltless. Jesus' coming was God in the flesh walking amongst man, fellowshipping with man, "eating" with man and meeting his needs. God embraced man, poured His love on man and most importantly closed the gulf between humanity and divinity. Christ dealt with the sin issue and this gave us access to and ability to stand before the Father again. This is why the veil in the temple was torn from top to bottom. I believe the tearing started from top so everyone knows man didn't tear this, God did! That action is significant in the sense that God wants everyone who accepts Jesus into their hearts to know that you don't need to come behind the veil to find me I would now live in your heart. It seems to me that with the tearing of the temple veil, the levels of intimacy have been opened to all regardless of when you confess your sins and accept Christ's sacrifice on the cross for you. It is no longer a question of when you became (or how long you have been) born again but of how much of God you truly desire to discover for yourself. God is saying "I would no longer determine how far you can come in your relationship with me. The veil is torn, and it is now in your hands; if you want to come deeper it is up to you" Every Christian can find God on the level he or she so desires for there are no restrictions anymore. From experience, I know God responds to every man on his level of hunger; if you desire more, you get more and if you desire none, you get none. It all depends on your level of hunger.

The bible tells us that God does not dwell in buildings or temples made with hands.

Acts 7:48
"However, the Most High doesn't live in temples made by human hands…" NLT

Acts 17:24

"The God who made the world and everything in it is the Lord of heaven and earth and does not live in temples built by human hands." NIV

Where then does He dwell? In the place crafted by the very hands of God; the heart of man. No wonder Paul says in 1 Corinthians 6:19 "Know ye not that your body is the temple of the Lord and the Spirit of God dwells in you?" The house of God (The Church) is not a building but the man who God sits upon the throne of his heart. God dwells in every believer "Be not afraid little children for greater is He WHO IS IN YOU than he who is in the world" 1 John 4:4. The building just makes it easier for the "Houses of God" to gather. This is why, it is when two or three are gathered in His name that He is present. For example, Anderson is a believer, Bukky is a believer and Ochuko is a believer. These three believers decide to meet in the building (what we call church) for prayers. The minute they walk into the building God is present not necessarily because He was there waiting but because they brought Him in their hearts with them. This is a profound truth which if understood and embraced, would revolutionize how you pray, work and live.

When I walk into a room, God enters because I brought Him with me. When I am alone and the devil whispers temptation into my ears or suggests it in my mind, I immediately relate with my divine side because wherever I am God is present. When I kneel to pray, I don't have to "feel a certain way" I just know I am in the very presence of my Father. Goose pimples in worship may not be evidence of God's presence. So also, swooning and "falling under the anointing" (as it is called) may not be the true evidence of God's presence. It is the deep conviction and realization that God dwells in me and practicing this truth daily that provides true evidence that God is present.

Therefore, when I work in a denomination, it is because I have Christ living in me that sanctifies (sets apart) the work I do and not the other way round. I can be in my secular work place; let's say on a drilling rig and still be "working for God". Because wherever I am, God is present and whatever I touch I sanctify (set apart) for God. Whatever we do is supposed to be a platform for God to be glorified. If I am singing in the choir or I am a dishwasher in a restaurant we can have the same effect. It all depends on who sits on the throne of our hearts and the motives for which we have been engaged. One is not more sacred than the other.

This is a major stronghold of organized religion because we have preachers on the one hand making people feel unfulfilled because they are not "working in God's house" and on the other hand making those who are workers in a denomination struggle with guilt because they cannot attend all meetings, always be at their duty posts and do all the head pastor or bishop wants because of conflicting demands in their secular worlds. It is funny that just the way we apply for jobs in the secular world, we are made to apply to work (serve) in God's house. So, we have classes that run into months to "teach" people how to behave in our denominations and what the expectations are. We tell them rules about this or that and "indoctrinate" them into the vision and mission statements of our denominations but we do not spend ample time telling them what Christ's dying on the cross does for them. Jesus in calling his apostles, simply said "follow me and I will make you…" The key is in following Christ because He does the making not man. Man's rules, doctrines and traditions do nothing but take away the liberty which allows a man to simply follow and become like Christ. So, we have people who seem to be "enslaved" and the genuine freedom in Christ isn't felt.

If these months of indoctrination was working as we hoped, why haven't we seen a steady decline in the cases of sin (especially sexual and financial sin) in the church? We focus on telling people what they can and cannot do instead of telling them who they are. If a man genuinely understands who he is he would know what he isn't allowed to do. Don't tell them who they are now because they have joined your denomination but who they are because they have joined Christ. Based on what the bible teaches, we have been joined (united) with the Lord and have become one spirit with Him. Do Christians in present day really understand the import of this statement in 1 Corinthians 6:17? This is what we should be showing and telling instead of focusing on making "loyal followers". The bible also mentions that we have been engrafted into God and are now partakers of everything that flows in the life-line of Christ. *"And if some of the branches be broken off, and thou, being a wild olive tree, wert grafted in among them, and with them partakest of the root and fatness of the olive tree;" Rom 11:17 KJV*

It does not matter how "wild" you were, soon as you recognize and believe you have been grafted in, you become a partaker of the nature of God and as such must live like God lived when He came in the flesh as Jesus Christ. It is this simple truth that brings change and empowers the new believer to live right. Not doctrines of dressing, living or denominational laws. It is this Truth that liberates. Jesus said, "I am the way the truth and life no man comes to the Father except by me" Truth and life are not Christian Doctrines Truth and Life is the person Jesus Christ.

So, when you are working in any organized establishment where Jesus is being preached, realize that you are working for the denomination and not necessarily God. How you handle the work you have been assigned to do is what determines if it will bring God glory or not. You can work for God even as a school teacher or cleaner. It's not a function of where you are but who you have become.

Then, one should be very careful when we take up assignments in our denominations because soon as we accept these roles, the challenge then becomes that God expects you to be faithful. This is what Paul was trying to emphasize in Colossians 3:23. Whatever you do, you must handle it like it is unto God. Like you were doing the work specifically for God. This is a good thing because whether we are in our denominational structures or in the corporate/secular world this is a principle that guarantees success. However, this has become part of the reason so many people are being abused in the Christian fold. Leaders put this verse in front of people to get them "scared-safe". People out of the fear of offending God, now do all they can to make these denominations prosper in their various works meanwhile their personal lives, intimacy with God and other demands God has on them continue to suffer. There exists then that false security that as long as I continue to help my Pastor in his denomination, I am working for God and God is pleased.

I fear that many sincere and genuine believers may find themselves on the wrong side of eternity not because they did not love God, but because they failed Him. Jesus showed us by the way He lived that, every man's priority in life must be to please the Father. Anything else is a complete waste of time. A man can work very hard in his denomination and end up outside of God's will for his life. Sadly, God will not accept as an excuse the fact that you were busy working for your denomination while His core assignment for your life suffered. *"It is the glory of God to conceal a thing: but the honour of kings is to search out a matter" Proverbs 25:2 KJV*

Our job is to find out exactly what pleases the Father and ensure we make it the priority of our lives as long as we still have breath in our nostrils. I say it again… anything else is a complete waste of time.

As at the time of my writing this, I have had people come to me sad and broken because of incidents that have happened within their denominations. The question on their lips the same "is serving God (or working for God) this hard?" One of those who came with questions; a brother, went ahead to say, "I fear that pastors and leaders have made Christianity so difficult for the average believer". These are the abuses "church workers" are facing in Christendom at the moment. No one cares how you pay your rent, if you can feed, what your challenges are, or how your spiritual growth is progressing. All they want is for you to give sacrificially, attend all meetings regardless of whether you have the means to or not, be at the beck and call of the denomination and live for whatever the denomination demands. So, we have people stretched thin trying to "please God" within their denominations but I fear that God is not pleased. When a man gives (be it money or time) what God accepts and honours is not just the gift but the heart with which it was given. That's exactly what Paul shows us by scripture.

2 Corinthians 9:7:
"You must each decide in your heart how much to give. And don't give reluctantly or in response to pressure. "For God loves a person who gives cheerfully." NLT

"Each of you should give whatever you have decided. You shouldn't be sorry that you gave or feel forced to give, since God loves a cheerful giver" GWT

It should NEVER be the denomination setting the standard for what is considered a good gift in cash or kind. It should be the believer. People are giving money and time to our denominations but are disoriented, disenchanted and grossly unhappy. Are we surprised that we cannot produce the same power in our denominations like the church of old? We should not be surprised. We have turned those who should cheerfully be serving God into disgruntled individuals who must do what they think they must do so as to please their church leadership and hopefully somehow please God. This abuse has got to stop if the church in my generation actually desires to make impact.

I hear some denomination leaders in Nigeria speak about not paying those who play music instruments in our sanctuaries "salaries" because in their opinion if a man wants to work for God he does not need to be paid to do God's work. Now apart from this being very wrong, it also sounds very selfish. What is the difference between the man who plays keyboard in the sanctuary and the man who has decided to go into "full time ministry" in any denomination? If we agree that it is okay to pay the Pastor who is in full time ministry salaries, then it should be okay to pay the keyboardist. Otherwise if one is a hireling then the other cannot be anything different since both are "working for God". The truth is religion has become a master in masking the truth (or better still bending the truth) to suit her purpose. The young man who plays keyboard probably has no other source of income and needs to take care of himself, family and maybe see himself through school. He is saved, sanctified, spirit filled, tongue talking, and demon chasing and wants to work. So, he comes and asks to play for your denomination (so he doesn't have to go and play in the clubs) so he can meet his needs and we tell him you should become a church worker and on and on so we can now put on him the working for God and no payment doctrine. If we believe God can provide for the keyboardist, the same God can provide for those in full time ministry too. If one deserves to be paid the other should not be criminalized or called carnal. Therefore, most Church people find unsaved persons playing music instruments and singing in our Choir. Is it not ironic that we send away those who are born again and then eventually end up hiring "anyone" to help us play the instrument? We want the best for our denominations, but we are unwilling to celebrate our own or pay the required price for the value we desire. So, people come in, pretend like they are one of us, ravish our sisters and daughters and pollute the atmosphere of worship in the church. I am a firm believer that those who play our instruments should be saved. This is non-negotiable. If the saved brother has a challenge and desires to be paid, then why not? If he suggests that out of love for His Saviour he wants nothing, then so be it! We should not stand aside and point fingers because service should be out of love and not compulsion.

Let me take this a little deeper even if I can hear the stones falling all around me. The truth is, if we can pay those who say they are in full time ministry every church worker should be paid. What is the difference between the man in full time ministry and the woman who has to close late from her secular job, run into church to sing in the choir, close late, come home to attend to her kids, sleep late in the night and wake up in the morning to start all over again? We are both working for God and should be paid. After all, the bible says "The labourer is worthy of his wage…"

This is critical because we have denominations where church leaders call meetings at will and keep people there for as long as they care to without recourse to the fact that some of these people have lives outside the church to manage. Some denominations have designed church such that there must be a meeting every day of the week. Not to mention those that happen monthly, weekly and/or quarterly. So, we have so many people struggling to have a proper work-life balance resulting in half-baked Christians who have no time for personal prayer or retreats, fellowship or encounters with God. Where is the time? When they spend everything trying to juggle denominational work and secular demands.

The problem is, for some, the church is already their place of work (where they are getting paid) so they do not bother staying there for as long as demanded - after all, that's where they earn their "daily bread". Unfortunately, others (who don't get paid by the church) are being made to feel like if they don't do this "work for God" then they are sinning against God and are not committed to the coming of the Saviour. No Sir! Being committed to the plans of a denomination is very different from being committed to the work of God. If I am of the latter, then I can rejoice but if I am of the former I better start preparing to be turned aside by the Master when the time comes.

An argument might be, after all nobody forces anyone to work in the denominations that have been put together and I agree. However, because we must gather, there would be need to have dependable people who can help with certain areas of our gathering. Where there is no order, there can be chaos which could lead to divisions and strife in God's family. This was the case that led to deacons being selected in the early church. As a Christian that loves God, one would naturally want to help; volunteer to help prevent chaos and disorder. This is what leads to many people committing to the work being done in our denominations. My argument is, we must not take advantage of this and begin to abuse people. Jesus clearly mentions this in scripture - The steward who begins to say that because his Master has gone on a journey and chooses to abuse the other servants under him, should be prepared for the wrath and judgement of the Master when he returns. I fear that this may be the case for many church leaders when our Saviour returns.

"And the Lord said, Who then is that faithful and wise steward, whom his lord shall make ruler over his household, to give them their portion of meat in due season? Blessed is that servant, whom his lord when he

cometh shall find so doing. Of a truth I say unto you, that he will make him ruler over all that he hath. But and if that servant say in his heart, My lord delayeth his coming; and shall begin to beat the menservants and maidens, and to eat and drink, and to be drunken; The lord of that servant will come in a day when he looketh not for him, and at an hour when he is not aware, and will cut him in sunder, and will appoint him his portion with the unbelievers." Luke 12:42-46

We have turned the Apostles doctrine upside down. In their day, everyone brought everything to the Apostles feet and it was shared to those who had needs. What we do now is, we take all the tithes and offerings and pay only select people in the church. Then we tell the church to source for other means to handle the welfare of those who have needs in the body. Where did we learn this? The problem is we became so organized that we need to take all the money to keep feeding our ambition instead of meeting the needs of our family members (church family) who have nowhere else to turn.

Acts 4:32 - 35 "And the congregation of those who believed were of one heart and soul; and not one of them claimed that anything belonging to him was his own, but all things were common property to them. And with great power the apostles were giving testimony to the resurrection of the Lord Jesus, and abundant grace was upon them all. For there was not a needy person among them, for all who were owners of land or houses would sell them and bring the proceeds of the sales 35and lay them at the apostles' feet, and they would be distributed to each as any had need" NASB

It doesn't surprise me at all that in the same discourse of sharing amongst the congregation of believers as we see above, we see the mention of great power being displayed as the apostles gave testimony (witness) of the resurrection of Jesus Christ. Our sermons lack power. We say we are believers, but no signs or wonders follow our preaching. At best in our denominations we have one or two men who are "managing" to produce very little supernatural results while the rest continue to struggle. Can our failure to follow the pattern set by the saints of old not be a contributory factor to this lack of power? I think we need to call ourselves apart and allow God deal with us on this.

Beloved reader, I am not in any way against paying salaries to pastors who have committed their lives to spreading the gospel. I know a lot of them who are doing this under conditions that are very challenging and deserve all the support (financially and otherwise) they are getting from their local denominations. Paul clearly states that "he who tends the vine, must be the first partaker of its fruit". He also says in *1 Corinthians 9:13-14 that "they which preach the gospel should live off the gospel"*. My discourse here is not to suggest that they should not be paid but to use this analogy to clarify the working for God concept in present day Christianity. I hope many would sit back, re-evaluate their position and do what God truly expects of us.

I love this scripture Mathew 25:31-46
"When I was sick you didn't visit. When I was a stranger you did not take me in or clothe me. When I was hungry you did not feed me. When I was thirsty you did not give me drink…. Get thee away from me I know ye not…"

Note that nothing is said about singing in the choir, ushering, preaching powerfully or attending church meetings. What we have termed God's work is not what God recognizes as His work. His work is to express His love to those who need to encounter Him. Men are to see God through us. If only this could become the central theme of the messages we preach in our sanctuaries. Our results in the world will astronomically increase.

This sounds blunt and rash but if we must kill religion and religious activity, the truth must be told.

I used that analogy, so I could move us closer to where I desire to go with this truth. Service in God's house should be borne out of love and nothing else. "If you love me, you would keep my commandments" Those were Jesus' Words. Love is the key… I remember a Senior Pastor I served under would always say "I would rather you provided yourself to work in God's house out of love and not because I would punish you". He never encouraged "punishing" church workers or ministers except in extreme cases where it involved sin. As relates to service and "working for God", it was always, "To yourself be true. If you love God, then help advance His kingdom through the work the denomination is doing". I was surprised to see the response this generated in the hearts of men. Love is indeed a powerful force.

For me, I believe this is a better approach and I can tell you people responded accordingly by attending meetings on time and providing themselves for service when called upon. What originates from the heart will reach the heart and what reaches the heart will produce far reaching results.

We should stop making God's people feel guilty because of certain assignments in our denominations. Sometimes when certain declarations are made or punishment meted out regarding attending meetings or doing one thing or the other in denominations, I just bend my head and ask "is this what God would have wanted?" Every time this hits my heart, the answer is always the same. I believe you too know the answer.

In fact, there have been cases where Church leaders have said to church workers "kneel down there" because the church worker did something wrong. Things that do not even happen in secular organizations have been brought into the Church. The worker most times kneels not only out of respect but because they have been taught that the work they are doing is for God so "I better kneel for God's sake". So, you have a married man with 3 children kneeling before his superior Pastor under punishment for doing something wrong. This is not right by God's standards and this is why people of the world look at us like we have lost our minds. People will say it means the man is humble but for me it is the leader emotionally abusing the worker in the name of religion. Let us call it what it is and not spiritualize "evil".

Jesus will NEVER have done that to any of His disciples. Again, this is where the problem lies; we say Jesus is our role model but Christian leaders say what He said but do not do what He did.
I know I would be reminded that God expects us to honour our leaders. And I agree completely. Let me show you some scriptures:

Hebrews 13:17
"Obey your spiritual leaders, and do what they say. Their work is **to watch over your souls, and they are accountable to God.** Give them reason to do this with joy and not with sorrow. That would certainly not be for your benefit." NLT

1 Thessalonians 5:12
"Now we ask you, brothers and sisters, to acknowledge those

who work hard among you, **who care for you in the Lord and who admonish you."** NLT

I would like you to read both portions of scripture again but slowly; with emphasis on the highlighted portions.

We have emphasized the first parts of this texts in organized religion. We are screaming on-top of our voices "Obey your leaders in God" "acknowledge them who labour amongst you". We drum this at every opportunity and at the "slightest provocation". People are told to submit to their leaders and obey absolutely. It now seems the flock are being examined; "if truly you are born again you will be humble and submit regardless of what the leader has done to you". My question is "what about the leaders themselves?" Have they done like Christ would have expected them to? Our first text clearly says they are accountable to God. If God were to weigh them in the scales would they not be found wanting? How many church leaders can truly boast that they are watching over the SOULS of those who have been committed into their hands? The emphasis should be on the souls of those who we are priviledged to lead but how many truly care about the souls of men? We say we care but our actions show otherwise. A man is not what he says. A man is what he does. What you do, defines who you truly are. As a church worker, pastor or minister in certain denominations, your soul can be famished up to the point of death and, yet there is no avenue for you to see the Bishop, General Overseer or Senior Pastor except you have connections at the top. These are things that are deeply troubling to me.

If we say we care for their souls, we would be very careful how we enforce what we call our denominational laws and doctrines. Our focus would be on encouraging the sheep to seek God and not putting stumbling blocks on their path in the name of discipline and commitment. Sometimes our actions (and inactions) have pushed the people farther away from God and generated resentment and anger in their hearts. This is the major reason for what we call eye-service in Christendom; the people seem to be working outwardly but inwardly they have lost genuine passion and love for what happens within the walls of our denominations.

Yes, the church leader cannot visit all the church members especially in a large congregation but what about the pastors and church workers under him? Does he know where they work? Does he know how they manage to survive? Does he know how they are faring spiritually? Does he know the battles they fighting? Most times all the church workers hear from their leaders involve, pay this money, sow this seed, pay your tithe, make sure you are in this meeting or that convention, gather for this program, dress in so and so way, make sacrifices for our denomination and on and on. Nothing about how their souls are faring. Too many church workers are disenchanted and frustrated. All they are doing now is staying put for God's sake.

The writer of Hebrew makes it clear; to receive honour you must be one who watches over the souls of the people under you. It seems to me that church leaders do not understand the tremendous value our Father – God places on a soul. Paul says in Thessalonians that before one can be acknowledged you must be one who cares and admonishes. We have left these two key assignments and focused on the rewards.

Now herein lies the danger; we are attempting to make withdrawals where we have made no deposits and this is what results in the resentment and hurt many church people are living with in this generation. People are no longer "serving God" with all their hearts. People are no longer giving whole heartedly. People are no longer advancing the kingdom in sincerity. Therefore, we have only a few people "sowing and reaping". The majority are just frustrated because it seems the more they give, the more the principle seems never to work for them. Principles are what they because they are expected to work every time. Regardless of where you are in this world or your status (rich or poor) if you plant any seed whatsoever, the result is growth. The seed does not pick and choose who to respond to because planting and harvesting is a principle. Instead of dealing with the issues causing resentment and frustrating the seeds that many genuine believers are sowing, we now turn and tell them they do not have enough faith.

There is so much eye-service and boot licking in today's organized church. So many men pleasers and few God chasers. We are making people serve God with so much deception; they are pretending like all is well but deep down they are complaining, grumbling and struggling to go through their days.
We cannot blame them because it seems the only way to survive is to do everything you are told without asking questions. To ask questions is to be seen as a rebel even when you see clearly that what is being done does not align with sound bible doctrine. Instead the church worker is told "if you want to work for God then you must follow this pattern or shut your mouth" or "If you want to go far in this denomination then do all you are told".

I fear that God is watching and waiting; at the end, we would know which was dear to His heart. To serve or to be served. We shall not wait for too long, for the day of our Saviour's return is near!
A brother or sister who decides to commit to helping the denomination's work grow should not be treated like trash or

made to feel like whatever they are doing there is for God. No, the believer should be treated with honour, love and respect. There is no place in scripture where it says if you are not a worker in so and so denomination you will not make it to heaven. Let people know that they can be in Church and still work for God wherever and however they choose. The man who is a doctor can make his hospital God's pulpit and use it to work for God. The engineer can do the same on a drilling rig. People should know that it is perfectly okay to come to church, sit in the pews, listen to God's Word, fellowship and go home. If you then choose to want to serve in any of the church ministries, then fine! However, you would be treated with love, respect and honour.

I have heard things like "I served during my time so I deserve to be served also" Beloved leader I ask you, would Jesus have made such a statement? He clearly showed the Father's pattern for greatness in John 13. If any would be great, he must serve. You served others yes I agree but these ones now with you where you are at this moment in time have you served them? Have you cared for their souls in ensuring they feel loved and are taught the bible (not denominational) doctrines? Have you labored for them in the place of prayer and love? Can they truly say "My pastor, bishop, Sunday school teacher or (whatever titles we bear) loves me? I wish we would focus on these things than making unnecessary demands on people who work in our denominations.

We have made Christendom a place where the leader is always right! We have told Church workers not to ask questions or "challenge" their leaders. We all must be YES-MEN and WOMEN. So even when we see that what is happening is wrong and unhealthy for God's people, we all must say YES SIR! I ask the church leaders who shepherd these flocks is this how God planned it? Paul says he challenged Peter before everyone when he saw Peter was erring.

Galatians 2:11
"But when Peter came to Antioch, I had to oppose him to his face, for what he did was very wrong" NLT

"But when Peter came to Antioch, I opposed him in public, because he was clearly wrong" GNB

Peter was eating with the Gentiles until some Jews arrived and he decided to withdraw. Paul saw this hypocrisy, publicly questioned it and rebuked Peter.

Jesus never shouted at His disciples for asking Him questions He answered everyone who came to him. Why are we making people in Church feel like they are in some kind of bondage? Christian leaders seem to be afraid of people questioning their decisions hence they send out signals like they have monopoly of God and he speaks to them alone. Any suggestion, question or remark from the followership is considered nonsensical. Like I said earlier, we have developed a protocol in ministry that shuts people up. Once the Pastor, Bishop, General Overseer or church leader says "God told me this is what we must do", everyone is expected to shut-up and follow – no questions asked. We seem to thrive on the "silence" and nowhere is this acceptable by God's standards.

This abuse of the Christian faith has continued to thrive majorly because of a lack of understanding; Lack of understanding like I have explained earlier, of where God's house is. When one genuinely loves God, and wants to help make the work of any denomination easier, such an individual will normally be willing to bear all just to keep doing something in "God's house". If we all know that singing in the choir is not necessarily working for God, we would live our lives better than we are doing now, especially outside of the sanctuary building.

Am I encouraging anarchy and insubordination in church? Never! What I am saying here is, we must have an atmosphere in our denominations that allows for people to question what we do without fear of reprisal or segregation. We must let people know that as leaders we are not beyond rebuke from anyone regardless of cadre or level on the ladder of life. We must let people know that God can speak to them too even though they are "just followers". I fear that church leaders feel if they take away the "mystery" surrounding their positions then their hold over the people will be broken. May I remind us that the mystery was never about the position of the apostles but because the presence of God was revealed by signs and wonders within the church. Fear came upon the people and no one dared to join them because of what they saw happening in their midst not because of who their bishop or general overseer was. See Acts 5:9-13. Organized religion has focused on titles and positions; emphasizing the need to honour men and titles while we have little or no genuine proof of the presence of God in our midst. Little wonder the world has lost the awe it once had for the church. We are no longer feared or held in high esteem. Anyone can come in to do, say and behave as he or she pleases. In fact, in present day, some church leaders are even being kidnapped.

Since we are on this matter, we might as well run full course. We say ours is a religion of love but alas our actions have shown differently. We claim to be doing the work of God but sadly most of what we are doing is oiling the machinery of our large "business" enterprise. This is a hard truth but it must be said…

Our pews are full of hungry people (yes, I agree Jesus said the poor you would always have amongst you) but let us be honest are we doing enough as a Church? We collect the "widow's mite" of these poor people in offerings and tithes but what do we spend it on? Larger auditoriums for bigger gatherings, salaries for full time minsters and any other thing we deem fit. Yet our churches are full of people struggling. It is almost hilarious at times when a church leader/pastor looks at someone who has no job, no means of income, struggling to feed and says "you will pay 20,000 naira for so and so project". A friend and brother of mine looked at one of his pastors speaking under similar circumstances and asked him "Please sir sincerely look at this congregation. Do you think these people can meet these demands?" Guess the response? "This is how it has always been done". We teach them that if the pastor lays such a demand, they should say "amen" and have faith. When the time comes and they default, we say their faith was not good enough.

Can we meet everybody's needs? No! But we can at least try! We can start by refusing to build auditoriums we do not need and focus on investing in the lives of our members. We can start by stopping all this organized offerings and collections and let people give out of love. Put the offering basket at the entrance and let people know if you want to give please do. We can show people the vision of the Church and leave them to God to tell them how and when to give instead of coming up with various erroneous theology of numbers and figures just to get the people to sow "special seeds" into our ministries. We can teach them why we believe tithing is good and use the tithe to actually bring "meat" to God's house.

Look at what happened in David's day. 1 Chronicles 29:1-9

"Then King David said to the entire assembly, "My son Solomon, whom alone God has chosen, is still young and inexperienced and the work is great; for the temple is not for man, but for the LORD God. Now with all my ability I have provided for the house of my God the gold for the things of gold, and the silver for the things of silver, and the bronze for the things of bronze, the iron for the things of iron, and wood for the things of wood, onyx stones and inlaid stones, stones of antimony and stones of various colors, and all kinds of precious stones and alabaster in abundance. Moreover, in my delight in the house of my God, the treasure I have of gold and silver, I give to the house of my God, over and above all that I have already provided for the holy temple, namely, 3,000 talents of gold, of the gold of Ophir, and 7,000 talents of refined silver, to overlay the walls of the buildings; of gold for the things of gold and of silver for the things of silver, that is, for all the work done by the craftsmen. Who then is willing to consecrate himself this day to the LORD?"

Then the rulers of the fathers' households, and the princes of the tribes of Israel, and the commanders of thousands and of hundreds, with the overseers over the king's work, offered willingly; and for the service for the house of God they gave 5,000 talents and 10,000 darics of gold, and 10,000 talents of silver, and 18,000 talents of brass, and 100,000 talents of iron. Whoever possessed precious stones gave them to the treasury of the house of the LORD, in care of Jehiel the Gershonite. Then the people rejoiced because they had offered so willingly, for they made their offering to the LORD with a whole heart, and King David also rejoiced greatly."

When one reads this, you can't help but notice the liberty and joy experienced herein. This same scenario in our denominations would have produced different results. Here we see a leader lead first by example. His passion for the temple was evident. He showed that his giving was born out of love and not "pressure from above". The people could not help but follow suit. It wasn't about what they would get from God in return it was an offering of love. This is the pattern we should be following but religion has brought "corruption and bondage" all in the name of being more organized.

It is funny how people will read this and say "This is just blabbing." If God is not pleased why hasn't He done anything?" Well I have learnt that results are not proof that God is pleased. It is not everything that works that God approves. Bro. Gbile Akanni put it this way "People may use different methods to get resources and those methods may seem to be working, but that does not mean they bear heavenly approval". I completely agree with him on this and if you have some doubt, you can ask our elder brother Moses who had a similar experience in scriptures.

God said "Speak to the rock" but Moses went out and struck the rock. Was there result? Of course, yes! But was the result proof that God was pleased? Emphatic No! Moses paid the price for that mistake and I believe many will enjoy the same fate except we turn from organized religion and begin to do true Christianity. The bible is VERY clear on God's expectations if only we would humble ourselves and admit we have made mistakes. God is always ready to help a man who responds to His dealings in their lives.

So, what does it mean to work for God?
I believe it will do us good to go back to Jesus and see His example. After all, He is the head of the church. Also, we might like to look at the lives of the apostles who pioneered the church dispensation ushered in by the resurrection of our Saviour Jesus Christ. Did they work for God? What did their working for God entail? Did it have anything to do with singing in the choir or being a member of the protocol team?

John 5:17 "But Jesus answered them, My Father worketh hitherto, and I work."

During His time on earth He regularly reminded us He was doing the work of His Father. When He said this, what exactly did He mean? Did it have anything to do with working in the synagogue or temple?

You might be tempted to say they had no need for organized singing or protocol in the time of the apostles and I would suggest that you are wrong. If they had need for people to serve tables, I believe there was also need to bring order to other areas of their gathering. I also like the portion of scriptures that say we should speak to ourselves in psalms, hymns and spiritual songs. It would suggest some form of structured singing and worship in our gatherings.

#1 Work – Believe
Someone asked this question in the scripture "What shall we do that we might work the works of God" and what was Jesus' response? This is the work of God…
John 6:28-29

"Therefore they said to Him, "What shall we do, so that we may work the works of God?" Jesus answered and said to them, "This is the work of God, that you believe in Him whom He has sent."
This is the work of God, BELIEVE IN HIM whom the Father has sent. Please go back and read that phrase again slowly. These Words were penned from the very mouth of our Saviour and Lord Jesus Christ. He didn't say preach the gospel neither did He say work in my vineyard. His response was simple; believe in Him whom the Father has sent. This is God's demand on your

life. Do you only bear the name of believer but do not really live the life?

What does it mean to believe? It means to accept something as true. So, Jesus is saying we must accept as true what He whom the Father has sent came to show us. This is critical because a man can never be greater than what he has accepted as true. Bottom line is you cannot be greater than your belief. You cannot say you believe in the one whom the Father has sent and yet He has no place on your priority list.

The depth of this then is, when your belief is correct, your service will be correct. We have tried to turn this around in organized religion. We are in a hurry to get people serving when we should be working hard to get them believing. Little wonder we are facing so many frustrations in our Christian faith. Our lives seem not to be experiencing the fullness of what Christ represents. Why? The just lives by His faith. What is faith? Faith is believing. Faith is the currency for living. Without faith, it is impossible to please God. Hebrews 11:6 "But without faith it is impossible to please him: for he that cometh to God must believe that he is, and that he is a rewarder of them that diligently seek him." KJV

So, it is very simple! To work for God is to believe Him. Believe He exists (that He is) and He rewards those who diligently come after Him (seek Him) with all their heart, soul and mind. God cannot do anything meaningful with or for anyone who does not first totally and wholeheartedly believe Him. What happens in Christendom is, we say we believe Him but our actions betray us. We claim to be living but we are dead; for the just must live by faith. This is the work of God to believe in Him whom the Father sent.

Mathew 15:8-9
"These people make a big show of saying the right thing, but their heart isn't in it. They act like they're worshiping me, but they don't mean it. They just use me as a cover for teaching whatever suits their fancy." MSG

Isaiah 29:13
"The Lord says: "These people come near to me with their mouth and honor me with their lips, but their hearts are far from me. Their worship of me is based on merely human rules they have been taught" NIV.

Most church people (or workers) I know have more belief in the things they have been taught by their pastors, bishops or general overseers than what God has shown by the Holy Spirit inspired Word. Some have more faith in handkerchiefs, anointing oil, holy water and other tokens than they have in the living Word of God. The average Christian when confronted with a challenge will rather bathe in olive oil than pour the Word over their souls.
Our Christian lives can never grow beyond our personal revelation of who God is. There are depths we can never truly

enjoy in our walk with and work for God until we set aside human rules and teaching that suits our fancy and come into a genuine experiential knowledge of God. Knowledge not born out of what we have been told but what we have personally experienced. It is this experience that births belief which produces outstanding results in the life of the believer. Anything else (or less) will birth positive confession which at best is powerless leaving the so-called believer empty handed; void of proofs.

This is what it means to work for God… Believe on Him who He has sent so that you can become a mighty tool in His hand to cause dynamic change in the world.

#2 Work – Reveal the Father's nature
John 9:1-7
"As He passed by, He saw a man blind from birth. And His disciples asked Him, "Rabbi, who sinned, this man or his parents, that he would be born blind?" Jesus answered, "It was neither that this man sinned, nor his parents; but it was so that the works of God might be manifest in him. "I must work the works of Him who sent Me as long as it is day; night is coming when no one can work. "While I am in the world, I am the Light of the world." When He had said this, He spat on the ground, and made clay of the spittle, and applied the clay to his eyes, and said to him, "Go, wash in the pool of Siloam" (which is translated, Sent). So he went away and washed, and came back seeing"

God's original plan for man did not include sickness, lack, pain or even death. These are as a direct result of man's disobedience in the garden and are considered the works of the devil. God's plan was for man to walk in this realm (the earth realm) as an extension of his Father-God. Man is made in the nature of God and created to dominate and rule over the earth and everything in it. Everything God made, He made for the enjoyment of man. Man was to live in plenty, enjoy good health and exercise dominion like His Father God. Dr. Bill Winston put it this way "God never intended for the world's system to supply the need of His family". God Himself supplied all that man would need. This is expressed when Peter says *"He has given us all things that pertain unto life and godliness"* See 2 Peter 1:3.

Man was made in the very nature of God. Sin came and destroyed this beautiful picture opening the floodgates for darkness, sickness, pain and death to thrive over man. It was normal for the disciples to ask Jesus the question they asked Him because they realized that sin opened the door to sickness; sickness isn't normal for man it is sin that gave it right to attack man.

My focus here is on Jesus' response. He said all that happened was so that the works of God might be displayed in the man in question who was blind from birth. What then is "the work of God" as mentioned here by Jesus? We see clearly that it is to reveal the nature of the Father.

Jesus says "everything that has happened is so that the works of God might be manifest. The word translated manifest also means revealed. Revelation only exposes what was already there. It is like when you have things in a dark room you won't be able to find anything until you turn on the light. The light made manifest what was there; it didn't make them appear it revealed what was already there. This is why He mentions in between "As long as I am in the world, I am the light of the world" I am here to shine into the darkness hanging over man such that the nature of the Father might be revealed through me. What is the nature of the Father? It is zoe; that eternal life that gives one power over the works of darkness. Restoring us to our original place in the hierarchy of the world. God (Father, Son and Holy Spirit) – Man – Devil, demons and others. In that order.

After He had spoken, He went ahead to perform a miracle by opening the man's eyes.

Jesus said "I must work for God while it is day because the night comes when no man can work". Notice that this had nothing to do with what we consider in present day Christianity as working for God. Jesus was speaking about revealing God's nature as Jehovah Rapha – The God that heals us.

Organized religion tells us it is okay to sing in the choir and yet not be able to reveal the Father's nature to the world. We are comfortable serving but we are not uncomfortable at our inability to work the works of God. Working for God means you are to shine his light into the darkness of sickness and disease. You are to reveal His nature daily. As long as you are in the world, the world must experience the Father's nature through you. This is what it means to work for God.

The nature of love, the nature of power, the nature of dominion and all that God represents must be experienced through us. It is sad to know that we can be in a room of Christians and yet not be able to tell the difference with the world. We talk the same, act the same, look the same and live the same. A wise man said "No one dare be so rash as to seek to do impossible things unless he has first been empowered by the God of the impossible". We seem to have received the Holy Spirit (baptism of power) but the world cannot point to proof of our influence over it. One of my senior pastors would always say "Go to my university and check. The ground (the earth) would testify I walked there". What a way to live! Can this earth testify that this generation of Christians walked here? We are "making noise" working in our denominations but the world is yet to experience the Father through us. I wish we would fall at the feet of our Master and cry for a new experience.

Everywhere Jesus went, He revealed the Father. This was His life's work; to reveal the Father. He said to the disciples "anyone who has seen me, has seen the Father". He came to shine the light of a superior kingdom and went about doing this daily. His influence extended beyond anything ever seen or felt before Him. Let truth be told: He came and did it as a man so we all would know; this is how every man born of God is supposed to live. One truth that must sink into the heart of every believer is, everything Jesus did on earth (including His death), He did and accomplished as a man. Scriptures tell us he emptied Himself of divinity (Philippians 2:7-10) so He could bring so many sons to the place called glory (Hebrews 2:9-10). When you accept this truth with all your heart, you would realize that you too can reveal the Father to the world at an even greater dimension than Jesus did. Remember He said "greater works than these shall ye do because I go to the Father" John 14:12. It seems He is saying, I have finished my own assignment now the stage is set for you to not only do likewise but produce greater results.

Where are the sons of God that the whole world is groaning for? We must manifest God's nature!
To work for God is to reveal His nature to the world.

#3 Work – Lost Souls
John 4:34

"But he said unto them, My meat is to do the will of him that sent me and to finish his work"

I remember the first time I came across the chapter where this verse was taken, I could not get my eyes of verse 4 "And He must needs go through Samaria." Jesus was compelled by something greater and deeper than we can describe to go through Samaria. It was of uttermost importance that He go through Samaria that's what verse 4 says. Now, when you read further, we find that He came to Jacob's well and encountered a woman. If you have ever been in Sunday school or church, you would know the story of the woman at the well so I would not go over the entire story (Can be found in John 4:7-29). What I want you dear reader to see from this is what led to Jesus making the statement in John 4:34 to His disciples.

Jesus was constrained by God to go through Samaria just to encounter one woman. A woman with a terrible past. One who would probably not have a place in some of our denominations in present day. The simplicity with which Jesus brought her to the experience of salvation would make all our worker's training within our denominations look more like what it is – indoctrination. Jesus showed this woman a simple principle; the work I have come to do, is to reach out to anyone God permits to come across me. You can drink of the living water and also bring others to drink of same. The woman left Jesus and immediately began to work the work of God. She went into her town and told everyone "Come see a man which told me all things that ever I did: is not this the Christ?" John 4:29. She seemed to be saying I have drunk of living water you too can come and drink. This has nothing to do with my denomination, general overseer or pastor this is the Christ! The theme of the message was Jesus! Are we then surprised at the result? Verse 30 says "Then they went out of the city and came unto him." All who this woman spoke to left everything they were doing and came to Jesus. What an experience!

We are singing in our buildings hoping that men will come to us but there are people going to the "wells" in our city hoping to find Jesus. The well could be a school, the hospital, the prison, the drilling rig, the market place or wherever it is that God has set-up for an encounter but we are comfortable in church. Well dressed and simply excited to have church!

Can we have such an experience in modern day Christianity? Where an ordinary woman after one encounter begins to work for God? The church would throw all kinds of hurdles in front of her to make sure she cannot just tell her testimony. We would immediately think of how to make her a baptized member of the church so she can begin to work for God in our denominations. Instead of exposing her to the Word so she can become a disciple who can disciple others. The Word of God is the only potent weapon in changing men. Everything else is just powerless ritual. This is why so many church buildings have become tombs. We have become a gathered people of "dead" men. Men who are consumed with exerting energies for a good course but in a wrong way. I fear this is why when we now come to God for answers in our lives we get none. We thought we were working for Him but alas we have left His work to suffer while we expend our energies growing bigger and better denominations. God cannot pay who does not work for Him.

When the disciples returned with food, Jesus was too excited to eat. He had done the work of God. He had worked for His father. When they pressed Him to discover why He would not eat, He spoke the Words we quoted from John 4:34. Permit me to put it in simpler form.

"I do not want to eat food. My food is to please my Father who sent me by doing and finishing His work."

If you do not understand what the Father's work is, you would think it means to work in a denomination. Jesus showed us with this example that it is to do God's will as it relates to lost souls. To do God's will means I must be where He wants me to be per time so I can encounter those lost souls whom He has a burden to save. This could be the classroom where I teach, the motor-park where I look for passengers or the oil rig where I do my work.

Too many souls around us are on a collision course with eternal damnation but we are in church (our various denominations) working.

The emphasis must change!

#4 Work – Full Assurance of Faith and Hope
1 Corinthians 15:58
"Therefore, my beloved brethren, be ye steadfast, unmovable, always abounding in the work of the Lord, forasmuch as ye know that your labour is not in vain in the Lord."

When one reads this verse of scripture we immediately think about the work we do in our denominations. While I agree that this verse speaks of Christian service, the focus isn't what we have made the central theme of this verse in organized religion.

To understand this verse in its entirety, I encourage the reader to begin at the very first verse of this chapter. You will find that Paul wasn't speaking about "working in the house of God" so this verse was not some conclusion on how to work in the house of God. This verse was a conclusion on an extensive teaching on life after death and resurrection.

Join me as we examine some verses preceding verse 58
1 Corinthians 15:51-57
"Behold, I tell you a mystery; we will not all sleep, but we will all be

changed, in a moment, in the twinkling of an eye, at the last trumpet; for the trumpet will sound, and the dead will be raised imperishable, and we will be changed. For this perishable must put on the imperishable, and this mortal must put on immortality. But when this perishable will have put on the imperishable, and this mortal will have put on immortality, then will come about the saying that is written, "DEATH IS SWALLOWED UP in victory. "O DEATH, WHERE IS YOUR VICTORY? O DEATH, WHERE IS YOUR STING?" The sting of death is sin, and the power of sin is the law; but thanks be to God, who gives us the victory through our Lord Jesus Christ.

The above is the reason Paul begins verse 58 with "therefore". He seems to be saying based on the above, be steadfast, unmovable, always abounding in the work of the Lord for as much as you know that your labour is not in vain in the Lord.

You must realize that Christ's victory is your victory! You must live in full assurance of faith and hope. If death could not hold Him, death cannot hold me. I too will resurrect into my original place in God. This then should be the motive for what I do here for God.

You see the difference? The emphasis is not in the work or labour but living in the consciousness of ultimate victory through Christ. The hope of the resurrection should spur us to do the best we can while we are still here irrespective of the enormous challenges we face. No wonder Jesus said "I must work while it is day. Night cometh when no man can work" I have a huge assignment for the souls of men but don't have enough time.

I believe Paul wants us to realize that we cannot be building permanent structures in a place where we are temporary residents. Our work should be focused on structures for where we will be permanently and not otherwise. Isn't it funny that we are expending our energies on activities that have no eternal value and our heavenly accounts are empty? Little wonder Paul says elsewhere, "set your affections on things above...."

Colossians 3:1-3
"If ye then be risen with Christ, seek those things which are above, where Christ sitteth on the right hand of God. Set your affection on things above, not on things on earth. For ye are dead, and your life is hid with Christ in God." KJV

Our affections, passions, strengths in modern day Christianity seems to be focused on things that do not add value to where we are going. Millions and billions are being spent on larger buildings, church programs and other things that makes one wonder if we still believe that this world is not our home and we are only passing through. Your work for God should be driven by this understanding and nothing else. My Father's work is immense and I don't want to be caught up in something that makes no sense in the long run.

From scriptures, we see that, not once can we find working for God to mean the things we do in present day Christianity. Be encouraged dear reader to also search the scriptures to see if this writer has erred in his conclusions. The explanations given have clearly been based on the experiences recorded in God's Word. I believe your search will bring you to the same conclusions the writer arrived at.

So where do we go from here?
The problem with organized religion is that we are now caught up as "zombies" in our posh sanctuaries working for God but God's actual work is crumbling all around us. Jesus said "the field is green with harvest. Pray the Lord of the harvest that He would send labourers into His vineyard." This is what it means to labour; to be out in the field "harvesting" the souls of men. The lost are perishing in the field of life and the saved are wasting away in their sanctuary buildings. We claim to be working for God but the results speak for themselves. Our church sanctuaries are full of "needy" people but heaven is empty of souls.

Our neighbours cannot experience God through us because we have not seen the need to work this work of God. We are fully dependent on pastors, prophets and bishops for the next word from God and yet our hope should be in what He has spoken in His Word. I fear we are raising a generation of Christians who are encouraged not to discover truth for themselves. They want healing but they don't want to pray. Oh, Pastor pray for me! Prophet please prophesy! Pastors have turned themselves into surrogate mothers when they should be midwives. A surrogate mother is a woman whom they take the seed from the man and it is deposited into her by a process called artificial insemination. She carries the baby for the couple and then gives the couple the child to raise. The problem with this is, there is a result but the couple never goes through the pain of the process. They don't know anything about morning sickness, they know nothing about the woman's fluctuating appetite, and they know nothing of the swelling feet, the pain and sometimes fear of losing the child. They only have the result but have never experienced the process. This is what happens in my generation - Pastors call people and say it is your foundation (as we like to call it in Nigeria. Family foundations, bloodlines and place of birth) but we will pray and God will do it. They rob these people of a personal experience with God. The challenge then is, when the storms of life arise the people are not able to replicate the result because they have no experience of the process and frustration sets in. The Pastor is supposed to be a midwife. The difference is, when the Christian is faced with an even worse condition, they have experienced the process and can reproduce the results because the pastor has only helped guide through the process while the "couple" have lived the experience.

When next someone is trying to make you feel the work inside the building is so important to God and your failure to sing in the choir, usher or "serve" the minister of God is a "sin", you need to refuse such erroneous teaching. Jesus clearly showed us what it means to work for God.

Preachers need to humble themselves and tell the people "join me so I can move this denomination forward" instead of hanging the working for God burden on the shoulders of men. Be sincere enough to admit we all have made mistakes and begin to take steps to correct them. People should fear and reverence God more than they do you. Stop threatening people into service. Tell them the truth and let them choose whether to stay or not.

Where am I going with all this?
Am I saying the expansion and growth of the church has been detrimental? No not at all…

Church expansion and growth has been of tremendous blessing. We have people listening to the Word of God in remote villages because of the efforts of certain denominations towards expansion and evangelism. More of the "unreached" are being reached because of the visionary work of so many denominations (including the one I belong to as at the time of writing this book) so I applaud the work the church has done. However, I am calling us back, to remember the essence of the whole expansion. It is not to make our denominations larger and bigger but to bring more people into God's family. We have focused so much on structures and figures that we have now begun to "enslave" those whom God sent to help fulfil His vision in our hearts. People are of the notion that soon as they can do some "good deeds" in our denominations then they have worked for God and can die happy. No... we must correct this.

If you did so well singing in the choir and never fulfilled your assignment as a doctor you have failed God. God wanted to do miracles through your hands and you "frustrated Him" by refusing to work for Him in this area of your life. God had children who needed to pass through your hands in the classroom but since you were too busy following your general overseer everywhere, you never got round to working for Him as a teacher in the classroom.

Invariably God will never allow His work suffer - We like to use this phrase when we speak of work in our denominations. The truth is when a man fails him, He finds another. Sad thing is sometimes when he looks within our organized religious circles and finds no man He can trust; He looks for a Cyrus outside. So, we have our heads buried in our denominations believing we are divinely useful but we have become earthly useless (or irrelevant) and as such God needs to find "stones" to further His work in science, technology, anthropology, medicine, education, politics, and other aspects of life. These aspects of life are platforms for God to glean the harvest that is ready.

These are truths church leaders must tell their congregations. Yes, it is nice to help this denomination achieve her goals but the work of God goes beyond this; God has needs we all must meet and He can use even our secular jobs to get men into His family. So, whether you are a church worker or secular worker none is more sacred than the other. The most important thing is if you are doing God's work with whatever platform He has provided for you.

Is it not sad that all church workers (and members) have become to their denominations are statistics? Denominations are "obsessed" with numbers; attendance figures, tithes and offering figures and in some cases number of branches established. This has become the emphasis. So, one can be in church dying spiritually and nobody will really care as long as the numbers and ratings continue to go up. One can be a novice (present day Christianity has mastered the art of crowning novices) in a position leading men and no one will really care as long as such work continues to add to the numbers in attendance and offerings. I ask you dear reader, how long will you continue to allow yourself be just a statistic? When will you arise and do the work of Him who called you? You are part of the called-out ones; the elect and cannot continue in cycles of religion and religious activity. Arise! There is nothing out there that can stop the one who aligns with the will of God for this generation. As at the time of writing this book, there is a massive shift in the realm of the spirit and a heavy outpouring of the Holy Spirit beckons... A great revival is at hand. Will you be part of it?

Christ said "He came to destroy the works of the devil..." 1 John 3:8

I have stated earlier that the works of the devil include sin and death and as the scripture above points out, Christ came to destroy the devil's work and He accomplished this task without leaving any aspect undone. Our job as believers is just to walk in this consciousness. We are not fighting a battle per se the battle has already been won. We are living the victory. Death has been dealt with; Jesus said he came to give us eternal life! So as soon as I become a part of the family, I have eternal life period! John 3:14-15 "As Moses lifted up the serpent in the wilderness, even so must the Son of Man be lifted up; so that whoever believes will in Him have eternal life."

1 John 5:13

"These things I have written to you who believe in the name of the Son of God, so that you may know that you have eternal life."
What is eternal life? That is the very nature of God; the very life of God; what we call zoe.

Jesus also dealt with sin no wonder John says *"he that is born of God CANNOT sin for the nature of God is in him"*
1 John 3:9
"Whosoever is born of God doth not commit sin; for his seed remaineth in him: and he cannot sin, because he is born of God"
1 John 5:18
"We know that whosoever is born of God sinneth not; but he that is begotten of God keepeth himself, and that wicked one toucheth him not."

Part of working for God is to believe these things that have been done, share them with others and bring them to also enjoy this victory purchased on the cross of Calvary for all mankind. Jesus said it is finished (accomplished); the work I came to do is done! A wise man said "Christianity is not performance; Christianity is believing, Christianity is beholding"

I sincerely pray that Christians all over the planet will indeed begin to work for God. May Christ indeed find faith on the earth when He returns!

WHERE HAS PASSION GONE?

One of the greatest foes of the Christian is religious complacency. The man who believes he has arrived will not go any farther; from his standpoint, it will be foolish to do so. – A. W. Tozer

Contentment with earthly goods is the mark of a saint; contentment with our spiritual state is the mark of inward blindness – A.W. Tozer

I was speaking with my younger brother who happens to be a minister of the gospel through music; one of the few I know who really know what it means to be in that ministry. We got talking about the issues I am raising here when he mentioned something profound. In this generation where we are "swimming" in organized religion, if we were to preach to someone who had everything; wealth, health, family, peace, joy and all you can imagine a man needs for his life to be complete. What would be the message?

I would like you to ponder on this carefully before we proceed. If you had all the money you would ever need, all the peace and security available, no issues whatsoever with your health, your family children and all doing well, would you have a reason to still pray? Would you feel desire or the need to be in church on Sunday morning? What exactly would be the message your pastor would preach that would be different from all you have been hearing regarding all the needs in your life? What exactly would you need to hear?

Why has this become an issue?
In the average church these days, the message is around God helping people from one thing or the other or God taking away poverty or God healing one sickness or disease or God delivering people from enemies and wicked men. So, what you have in church is a bunch of passionless and needy people. These are supposedly saved and sanctified people; born into the family of God. But it seems the emphasis that brought them was distorted. The message they heard "that convicted them" was based on what God could give and not who He is. This is not necessarily a "bad thing" because when we read scriptures we see people who came to Jesus because they had needs and desired his help. But in present day this becomes a challenge because the man who is "enjoying" his life in the world looks in the church, hears the message and says "I don't need their God because what they say He can give, I already have or worse still I can get in no distant time". Why then should I join them to "give my life to God?" If all that my believing and giving will produce are the things I can get by remaining on this side of the fence.

We have consistently preached this half-truth making it the central theme of our gatherings. I call it a half-truth because on its own it does not bring the freedom that Christ says knowledge of the truth brings. Yes, God wants us healed, rich, and prosperous but beyond all of this God wants us to become like Him in every area of life. This is the ultimate goal of the Christian faith. I see Jesus speaking in Mathew 5 showing us certain standards and exposing God's expectations to us. He seems to be saying "when God comes looking for you, He looks for sincerity but when He has brought you into His family, He expects perfection". Mathew 5:48 "Be ye therefore perfect, even as your Father which is in heaven is perfect." Yes, God wants to give us gifts but greatest of all, He wants to give us Himself. To drive the best cars, live in the most beautiful houses, build the largest auditoriums in the world and not get people to meet this crucial expectation of God is at best nothing but religion and not authentic Christianity. The bible is very clear... I didn't write it.

Organized religion needs this half-truth message, so we can keep the people locked in our church buildings. It seems to be some kind of hypnosis, so the people do not wake up. The people are trooping into our buildings but lacking life and passion for whom they should be seeking. I will like the reader to reflect on the messages (Sermons) he or she has heard in the last one month (or even one year) in the denomination you attend. I will also like you to reflect on the prayers that you have been a part of in the last one month. What have been the central theme of these meetings/gatherings? Honestly did you find God the last time you were in church? Have our seeking and praying not been around the things we can get from God? Have the prophecies not been about how God will attend to one matter or the other in our lives? When last has the focus been on God personally dealing with us to bring us to the place of perfection?

One must realize that reaching perfection is not something a man can achieve on his own. This is what I love about God. He sets the standard and still provides the grace (enablement) for us to meet the standard. God knows we cannot reach this point or become like Him on our own so He provides us the means to do so by giving us the Holy Spirit to work within us. Changing us from the inside out that we might indeed become perfect even as our heavenly Father is perfect.

The birth process for most of those who have joined the family of God has been in this manner: They hear a message on healing, deliverance, wealth or whatever the pastor may choose, and they are told if they want to enjoy these benefits in their lives, then they must shun their evil ways and come to God. At this call, many troop to the altar; some even with tears in their eyes and quickly the usher is called to count and give cards so at our next ministry meeting we may announce "1 million souls have been won"

The problem with this is, millions of children have been born and all through their life time their focus is on what the Father can give and not the Father Himself. This is the major contributory factor to the passionless empty Christianity we now witness in this generation.

Men come to God because they want to be healed, delivered, fed and clothed and not because they recognize deep down that apart from God, life as we know it indeed is meaningless. So, these crowds continue to come to gather in their large numbers at our special programs seeking what they believe they should get from the Father. So, they come for miracles, they come for financial breakthroughs, they come for one need or the other but do not come for God. This is why after a while, they are frustrated, dissatisfied and end up depressed. These "needs" can bring us to the feet of the Master but ultimately what will satisfy our longing souls must go beyond our needs being met to Jesus being revealed in us.

I remember back in the day when we were in university we could give up food just to be with the Lord. Some of us were prepared to stand on "mountain tops" to proclaim the love of Jesus. Our lives were sold out, our hearts on fire and our yearnings and desires wrapped around doing that which pleases Him who has called us out of darkness into His marvelous light. We would come into a worship service and be completely lost at His feet; tears streaming down our cheeks as we behold the beauty of His face. We didn't care if people called us fanatics or crazies we just poured our love on Him. Nothing else mattered but to passionately pursue hard after Jesus!

I was speaking to a senior minister in my denomination and he said "people don't like stayin for long periods in church these days. In our own time, we never wanted church to end" He was trying to tell me that back in his day, when they were in church, they were willing to spend hours in the church building and around God's people. I sat back and thought about this. I realized that when compared to his day, our message in present day is different. Back in the day the focus was on getting to know Jesus personally and impacting others for the kingdom. No one was concerned about how much was in their bank account or when the next meal will be provided. Men and women were completely sold out to the teaching and preaching of the gospel of the kingdom. Today the story is different; our focus in on how we can buy new cars, kill all the enemies in our father's house and make all the money in the world. Little wonder men no longer have passion for our meetings.

It is troubling now when I walk into Church services or meet church folk. Christians are more concerned about what they can get from God than what He demands of us as His children. Churches now focus more on "fire "and deliverance and we see Christians in a mad rush to get "delivered". Church services are laced with acrobatics; people falling all over the place in the name of "a special move of the Spirit". Because the average Christian is always seeking some form of validation; something to prove that indeed the man of God is anointed, preachers in present day will do anything to make people "fall under the anointing" including pushing people's heads. We have majored on externals while the secret life of the believer is left to rot. We come to Church not to see Him and fellowship with Him but somewhat to get something off Him. I keep asking where the passion has gone.

I long for a change to see us walk into Church services and experience the presence of God in true heartfelt worship. I long for a time when the Church will be more concerned about influencing this generation for Jesus than killing demons. Honestly, I'm tired of hearing the Nigerian church shout fire! Or Die! Die!! Die!!!

I call on Christians to arise and bear fruit. You were placed here by God to influence your world.

John 15:1-8 MSG
"I am the Real Vine and my Father is the Farmer. He cuts off every branch of me that doesn't bear grapes. And every branch that is grape-bearing he prunes back so it will bear even more. You are already pruned back by the message I have spoken.

Live in me. Make your home in me just as I do in you. In the same way that a branch can't bear grapes by itself but only by being joined to the vine, you can't bear fruit unless you are joined with me.

I am the Vine, you are the branches. When you're joined with me and I with you, the relation intimate and organic, the harvest is sure to be abundant. Separated, you can't produce a thing. Anyone who separates from me is deadwood, gathered up and thrown on the bonfire. But if you make yourselves at home with me and my words are at home in you, you can be sure that whatever you ask will be listened to and acted upon. This is how my Father shows who he is—when you produce grapes, when you mature as my disciples"

In Christendom, we have used the above scripture to suggest that when Jesus speaks of bearing fruit, it means we are expected to win souls for the Kingdom. Though soul winning is a very critical and important aspect of the Christian faith, that is not what Jesus was speaking about here. First, fruit is not something that is external to a branch. Fruit is something that comes from inside of the branch. To say then, that when I go out to win souls I have borne fruit in accordance with this scripture is not totally correct. The emphasis here is on the outflow of the supernatural life which lives in us as we connect (or are joined) with the vine – Jesus. So, what Christ was trying to say to us here is, as we abide in Him, His life flows through us and men are supposed to see the fruit of the supernatural life in us as Christians. We cannot be connected to God and not be able to produce His nature. If we grew out of Christ (as the branch grows out of the vine), we are expected produce the very nature of God in this realm as His children. Hence, He says "He that abides in me and I in Him brings forth much fruit". Meaning that I cannot separate His nature from His ability. If I abide in Him and His life flows through me, then everyone must see the fruits expressed in things like the wisdom and love of Christ, His power and anointing and the way I relate with my fellow human beings. This is the fruit Christ speaks of here. Abiding connotes spending long periods in the secret place with God so we might effectively represent Him in the world. The Father is glorified when men can experience God through us. This is the proof of discipleship; that you have been with God and now live like Him in this realm. As Christians, we are meant to be portals through which the love and power of God is released in this realm. This is how God shows who He is; that He can take an ordinary man, be joined to him, and through him produce supernatural results. The flow of GENUINE spiritual power can only come by being joined to Christ on an intimate level. Like the translation above put it, separated from Him we are nothing but dead wood – void of the nature and ability of God.

May I remind you that the bible says ye are the light of the world and ye are the salt of the earth? Beloved, get on your knees, ignite your passion, pursue hard after God and become His vessel in this generation. You cannot be satisfied with an ordinary mediocre Christian life. Why should I choose to be (or become comfortable with being) dead wood when I can be the very extension of God in this realm? Oh, Holy Spirit... Set me on fire from the inside!

I am not saying we all have got to be Pastors.... No not at all! But I know we all are placed here to create dynamic change. We can only influence this generation and bear fruit if we are under a greater influence! Nigeria currently needs passionate men; men full of God and ready to influence this nation for Him. Sadly, most Christians in Nigeria would rather be in their various church buildings singing and dancing.

Get hungry for something different dear reader and passionately pursue God! CATCH THE FIRE!!!
What has happened to "Oh king, we are not careful to answer you on this matter: Our God whom we serve is able to save us from thine hand and even if He doesn't save us we will not bow" Daniel 3:16-18

The passion of the three Hebrew boys is evident to all. We are not after what He can give we are after Him. Can we truly say the same about our large congregations? Even though God doesn't do this thing I am asking for I will keep pursuing Him? Can this truly become "a song" on our lips? Most people who call themselves Christians are not satisfied with having God alone. They desire the perks that come with the relationship more than the essence of the relationship. I believe strongly that God will only trust certain men with all He can give. Men who have become satisfied with Him as their all in all. As a song writer said "don't give me a mansion on top of a hill, don't give me the world with its shallow thrills. Just give me a savior; my life He can hold.

I would rather have Jesus than silver or gold" Just give me Jesus... everything else can wait! Hallelujah!

When people "give to God" in our churches what exactly is the motive? Is it not so God as an "honest business man" may give them in return one million-fold? When they come to programs even on Sunday mornings is it not so that the week beginning Monday may provide them some favour? Our people no longer come to our church buildings to find God, they come to find what He can give hoping somehow that with those things they get, they can validate the experience as one in which God was found.

Passion for God and His face is what He desires. Nothing else will be good enough!

No matter how much work we say we are doing within our denominations, if we do not bring the people to a place of a passionate pursuit for God we have failed terribly. I need not remind you that God says "seek ye first the kingdom of God..." It would seem to me that He does not tell us what to seek second because if we get the first right, every other thing would normally fall in line.

Organized religion has helped define what should be first for the Christian community knowingly and/or unknowingly.

Every time we prioritize church buildings over the lives of men we have made an explicit statement to the world. Every time we seem to put God up for sale with our words or deeds we have made an explicit statement to the world. Every time we choose to compromise godly standards we reveal to the world where our hearts truly are. Every time we get the opportunity to care for the souls of men and we fail in our responsibility we have made a very bold statement to the world. And I dare say God will hold us accountable. We are all after all accountable to Him.

Where has passion gone, I ask? Where has it gone?
We have driven passion for God and His face out of churches with our organization and structures. We teach people to preach in a certain way, talk in a certain way, act in a certain way; we create clones of our general overseers and senior pastors not knowing we have begun to restrict the flow of the Holy Spirit. A man preaches a certain way and we say "Pastors in our denomination don't talk like that" In the name of organization and structure we kill spontaneity and originality. So, unlike the days of old when the Spirit of God could show up how and when He wanted to, now He might need permission from the senior pastor or general overseer before he "interrupts" our church services.

I have been in meetings where in the middle of worship a senior pastor walks in and everything must stop to recognize his presence regardless of what was going on before he or she came in. So, whomever is leading the worship stops and hands over the microphone to the senior pastor so he can pass across some "very urgent" announcement or whatever brought him. My pain with this is that the leaders think this is correct. How can we be in the middle of worshipping God and we stop just to take announcement or acknowledge the presence of a man? These things are baffling not necessarily because they happen but because we have now made them into a standard, accepted them as normal, and teach them to the ones who are coming behind us. Oh, dear senior pastor who are we to fear more? You or God? There is a complete disregard for the ministry of the Holy Spirit in present day Christianity. There are things we are doing now that if anyone had attempted them in the days of the Apostles, it would have meant instant death. We trivialize these things because we are in a dispensation where God has decided to be gracious to us.

Unfortunately, religion and her associated activity like what I mentioned above have driven passion from within the walls of the sanctuary. When those in the pew see things like these happening, those of us who should know better without saying a word have told them what we think is more important. I remember when a brother called me and said "Pastor what happened when you were away is simply not correct" I responded by asking "what happened?" and he went ahead to describe to me how the minister on duty had started preaching the Word of God when suddenly a senior pastor arrived. He had to stop the message mid-way so an announcement can be made by the senior pastor. I was heartbroken! God was speaking to His people and we interrupted such a discourse to honour a man? Imagine this happening in the day of Moses at the mount. God would have struck such a man dead instantly.

Even if you feel the person who is preaching, leading worship or doing whatever thing is so little compared to you, one must learn to respect God regardless.

Dear senior pastor, general overseer, bishop etc., we must remember that we are not the message. You are not the reason men gather in the sanctuary. God most remain the central theme of the message. You cannot barge into a service half way, take people's eyes off God and fix them on you. PLEASE, enough of this religion!

We have driven passion away with our falling standards. Now women can dress half naked and speak in tongues on the pulpit. I was watching a major Christian network some years ago, and had to run to another station for my dear life. The woman on the altar had all her breasts out in full glare yet she claimed she was teaching the scriptures. It wasn't long after I read her marriage had broken up because of a reported adultery on the part of her husband. When you are showing what should belong to your husband to other men to feast on freely the same "spirit" will make your husband go feast on other women freely.

I remember I was in a church for a vigil one night. I had arrived to speak for the man of God. By the grace of God, I had been waiting on God and was looking forward to a wonderful meeting. As I walked into church and took my seat in front I was shocked at what I saw. There on the altar leading worship was a young girl whose clothes were all see through. I looked around and noticed she was the only one who seemed to be "in the spirit" as everyone else was just cold. You cannot be under the influence of the spirit of seduction and attempt to bring down the presence of God.

The spirit of seduction has taken over the church and we are celebrating it. Worship leaders stand on God's altar seductively dressed and claim to be leading us into God's presence. Let us be real with ourselves. If Jesus were with us in modern day, sitting on the front row, what would have been His response to these things? We do not have to scratch our heads to find out. We can see, from the way He responded to money changers and those who were buying and selling in the temple, He would have brought out a whip and flogged those half naked and "poorly" dressed women off the altar of God.

In some of our denominations we are "afraid" to talk about it lest we are seen as not contemporary. My younger sister told me of a mega church in Lagos Nigeria where as she entered she was shocked to see women dressed like they were going clubbing on Friday night. They claimed to be coming to God but were dressed in seductive robes on Sunday morning. Yes, all have been invited for the feast but we must remind ourselves that all are expected to wear the wedding garment. Mathew 22:11-12 *"But when the king came in to meet the guests, he noticed a man who wasn't wearing the proper clothes for a wedding. Friend,' he asked, 'how is it that you are here without wedding clothes?' But the man had no reply."*

Even though this passage speaks about the garment of righteousness, I would like to use it to buttress my point as we confront the spirit of seduction. All through the bible God's standard is very clear – You cannot dress like a prostitute and be speaking in tongues. Our sister's skirts, blouses and trousers are tighter and skimpier than what even people of the world wear. Which Holy Spirit did you receive that didn't tell you "my daughter, this dress is too tight or your top has been cut too low exposing your cleavage? Just like the man in the scripture above was speechless; he had no reply meaning he was without excuse. So, we all would be when He faces us with the same question. Thou art inexcusable oh church leader. There is no reason why women young or old should be advertising their bodies within our sanctuaries. There are "wedding clothes" and all must be properly dressed! If not, just as the man was cast out, not just those who have refused to dress properly but also those of us who have celebrated them by giving them place on our pulpits shall receive from Him "get thee away from me, I know ye not"

A Christian woman does not need to look "sexy" or "hot" she needs to look godly. *"Likewise also that women should adorn themselves in respectable apparel, with modesty and self-control, not with braided hair and gold or pearls or costly attire, but with what is proper for women who profess godliness—with good works." 1 Timothy 2:9-10 ESV*

That's God's standard. Are we then to drive them away when they come? No, not at all! We must however show them the correct way by preaching God's standards to them without fear or favour.

There are two extremes to this. On the one hand, we have the extreme as mentioned above and on the other we have those who have now made it a constant sermon on their pulpits how that a woman should not wear a man's clothing and vice versa. Is this in scripture? Yes, it is and we must obey the bible... Deuteronomy 22: 5 "The woman shall not wear that which pertaineth unto a man, neither shall a man put on a woman's garment: for all that do so are abomination unto the LORD thy God."

We pick this verse and try to "enslave" people in organized religion. What exactly categorizes male or female clothing? How did you come to know which was for men and which should be for women? Beloved child of God, the emphasis in this verse is "what pertains to a man or woman" the key word there is pertains. What does this word mean? The dictionary defines it as be a part of something. Synonyms include refer, relate, and have to do with. This verse is saying a man must not wear what has to do with a woman and vice versa. If a trouser has been made for women, then it pertains to a woman. If a skirt has been made for a man, then it pertains to men. This is exactly the case in Scotland where the men wear what is called a kilt. Would we say our Scottish brothers who dress up in kilts when the need arises are abominations unto God? The kilt pertaineth unto men and not women. Or in my Urhobo culture when I wear my wrapper as a man I probably should be considered an abomination unto God because the wrapper essentially is for women. No Sir! The wrapper pertaineth unto men in that case.

Wherever you go, people should be able to look at the way you dress and by your clothing be able to tell you are a man or woman. Per what is acceptable within your culture, a man should always look like a man and woman like a woman. A man should not go and take what has been attributed to women and begin to wear and likewise should a woman not do the same. Whatever has been set aside as related to any particular sex (male or female) should be treated as such. Therefore, I would not wear my wife's wrapper I have my own.

Even though traditionally trousers (or pants as some call them) are attributed to men, any student of history will tell you women in certain cultures have been wearing trousers since long before many of us reading this were born. So, we should not say the trouser has always been clothing for men alone. That would be incorrect. History is there to be studied; we all can verify. We suddenly evolve and say it is no longer women's clothing and whoever wears such is going to hell? No sir! That is not scripture. I wish we would approach all the erroneous teaching in organized religion with the same vehemence and passion we have approached this matter of men and women clothing.

We miss what God was trying to do here with his people. In bible times, trousers were not worn by either sex so this cannot have been what God was pointing out when he raised the issue of cross dressing with the Israelites. He was trying to address the spirit of homosexuality, lesbianism and transgender. He seems to be telling His people, you must not allow this demon into your midst by what you do; a man trying to look like a woman or a woman trying to look like man because all who attempt to do this not only become subject to this spirit (homosexuality, lesbianism and transgender), but also become abominable before God. The spirit of homosexuality, lesbianism and transgender are already flooding the church in present day and if we are honest with ourselves, it has its roots in a man wanting to look like and have what a woman has (and vice versa) which is what God was pointing out to His people Israel. Probably we need to begin to focus on addressing this instead of building doctrines around what is "unnecessary".

Our focus or emphasis should not be the clothing but decency. We should teach the people how to hunger for God. I am yet to meet anyone who truly encountered God and it did not affect their entire life including how they dress. A man who has an ear ring and piercing in his ear comes to your church and you think by attacking him with hell fire he would change? No sir! Show him the Word, get him to encounter God and you would see what happens thereafter.

Any preacher who continues to say people who wear trousers and those who do not cover their hair are going to hell needs to go back to God. That is not scripture. And I dare the preacher to go back and ensure he reads and obeys ALL the bible has written without interpreting it correctly and see where it would take him or her. One that readily comes to mind is below:
Exodus 20:26
"And do not approach my altar by going up steps. If you do, someone might look up under your clothing and see your nakedness." NLT

Simply put, all those churches whose altars have steps are erring against God and will soon face judgement. Because the bible clearly says "you must not approach my altar by going up steps". I can easily start a church doctrine from here in organized religion and have a wonderful scripture from the mouth of God Himself to back it up. So, I get everyone to begin to break the steps on their altars because our nakedness could be exposed. Especially our wives who wear skirts and climb the stairs.

You see how easy it is to take something out of context in scriptures? To understand what God was saying here we must go back to study correctly what God was saying to His people here, what Aaron and his priests were wearing, what the altar represents and ask the Holy Spirit to open God's heart to us. I leave that to you who reads to study, pray and make your conclusions.

We cannot pick and choose. If we say "obey the bible as it is" let us not choose the verses which to obey. It is all or nothing! Rather I say we must teach our people how to desire personal encounters with God, be filled with His Spirit and passionately pursue Him. The result will be total transformation within and without our denominations.

Just in case you are wondering, trousers are not part of my wife's options when choosing what to wear out; to church, work or wherever. So, this is not a defense she simply doesn't wear them not because she fears hell but because she just doesn't like to. It is based on her own personal convictions as God revealed Himself to her. I know there are some sisters like that who have never worn one all their lives not because they are afraid of hell but just because they don't want to for whatever reason.

I am not saying we should throw caution to the wind. At least my thoughts were clear in analyzing the other side of this coin. I do not believe a man should be wearing earrings or dressing like a woman. I certainly am appalled when a woman dresses like she has planned to "upset" all the brothers in church. What I am saying is, if we focus on discipling the people to become like Christ, it will reflect in how they dress. A woman who knows her body is the temple of the Holy Spirit will not dress in revealing or tight clothes. She would know God demands decency and modesty!

We have driven passion away and if we do not get men back on their knees crying for God and God alone, we would of our own be destroying our denominations from within.

Salvation is meant to produce in us an insatiable hunger for God. Instead what we see in our modern-day Christianity is when men get saved we indoctrinate them instead of setting them free to pursue deeper intimacy with the Father.

People pouring into your meeting in their millions is not proof of passion. People confuse the coming of the crowds as proof of hunger for God. Jesus put this succinctly when he said you are not coming because you want the Word of life, you are coming because of the bread that filled your belly. See John 6:26. Crowds can gather for anything that satisfies and excites the flesh but few men are found in the place where passion actually calls. The god of entertainment has taken a stool in our denominations so we do anything possible to get people to gather in droves. So, we do not mind if the comedian who we invite is "lying" we say no it's not a lie we are only joking... so people can laugh! We advertise retreats and crusades and throw in pictures of popular comedians on the banner for good measure. Anything to get the crowds to come. When people on the outside see the crowds trooping in, they mistake it for passion. Passion seeks for God and who He is not necessarily for what He can offer. Until we raise people who are sufficient enough and satisfied with God alone despite the obvious lack of other things, we continue to swim in the waters of religion. God honours passion for Him and His face. Every other hunger is secondary. This is why many leave the church service dissatisfied. They saw the advert, they came for what the pastor had to offer and when they left they were surprised that the entertainment was still not enough to fill the emptiness they felt. The souls of believers are famished and dying of hunger yet we are feeding them excitement and entertainment in church!

I have walked this road before and I must say I deeply regretted the experience. I organized a special program tagged "Laugh and Be Healed". I did my best to pull comedians from far and wide. The lead comedian I contacted for some reason arrived late and I found myself at about 12am going to pick him up from the bus station where he was dropped off. As if that stress was not enough, I didn't know I would have to contend with other aspects of this road I chose to travel. The program began at about 4pm later that day and I was surprised to see other comedians coming to my church. I was shocked! Most of these people (obviously unbelievers) yet they were arriving in my parish to "minister". When I watched the video some days later, I was pierced in my heart and I vowed never again to make the Lord's altar a place for worldly entertainment. This is the response I hope this book will generate in the hearts of our church leaders. We must call ourselves to order, we must speak the truth to our hearts and take appropriate action to correct the anomalies in our denominations. The longer we allow this complete disregard and dishonor for the Holy Spirit to continue, the farther we drift from the Father, His will, plan and purposes.

The scriptures are very clear:
Ephesians 5:3-4
"But fornication, and all uncleanness, or covetousness, let it not be once named among you, as becometh saints; neither filthiness, nor foolish talking, nor jesting, which are not convenient: but rather giving of thanks"

Ephesians 4:29
"Let no corrupt communication proceed out of your mouth, but that which is good to the use of edifying, that it may minister grace unto the hearers"

God's altar is not for comedy we must go back and cry to Him to set our hearts right. We are trying so hard to become like the world so we would be accepted but we forget we have been called out, separated, chosen and set apart for God. We are not meant to fit in, we are supposed to naturally stand out!
Christians praying in seeming fervency in the corporate gathering is not a proof of passion.

In Nigeria, most of the times when prayers are led in the corporate gathering, we have the person leading the prayer say "repeat after me... Father!" and every one repeats. After which the details of the prayer point are called out (with everyone still repeating) and then we are left to pray. Now because everyone is shouting and repeating after the prayer leader, we confuse this for fervency and passion in prayer. I personally have seen people shaking their heads vigorously in prayer and when I move close to hear what is being said, they are only mumbling senseless nothings yet when the man on the outside sees all the shakings, ramblings and shouting it is mistaken for passion. I saw a video once from one of the major denominations in Nigeria and the way a certain brother was twisting, bending, shaking and turning in prayer I cannot even describe with words. I only shook my head; religion yet at work!

Passion is like a fire in the heart; you seem to know what you are feeling but cannot describe it with words. You are praying, tears are running down your cheeks, and you find yourself speaking from a place in your heart you never knew was there. Prayer isn't in the multitude of words but in the sincerity of the experience. Prayer is not in shouting or shaking. Prayer must first be the posture of the heart; It is the heart of man reaching the heart of God. This is the kind of prayer that actually produces results. What makes prayer powerful is not vain repetitions or plenty speaking but in gaining alignment with God's will. John put it this way "And this is the confidence we have in Him, that, if we

ask anything according to His will, He heareth us". 1 John 5:14
One of Job's friends seem to have found this out and shared same with the man of God as he went through his trials

Job 8:5-7
"If you will seek God and plead with the Almighty for mercy, if you are pure and upright, surely then he will rouse himself for you and restore your rightful habitation. And though your beginning was small, your latter days will be very great."

A lot of the praying we are doing in Christendom is producing so little results because the lives of the men and women doing the praying are not correct and in alignment with God. If only we would be pure and upright, then God will rouse Himself for us and answer our intercession and supplications. We want to experience the power in answered prayers but are unwilling to allow God work in us so our lives will be correctly positioned in Him.

Please read what the Holy Spirit dropped in my heart – the church is supposed to be a place where people's passion for God is kindled. People are supposed to come into our services to find God. Hunger for Him, His face and His heart are supposed to be the central theme of our messages. People should know that, first before anything, they need God not because He can take away poverty or heal their bodies but because our being is incomplete without Him. Man was created to give God pleasure. So, man is incomplete without God.

I believe strongly that if we change the emphasis, passion and joy will return to the church. People now are just managing to go through church because there is nothing exciting about coming to church anymore. People don't wake up with an anticipation as they prepare for church services; going has become to fulfil all righteousness. This we must change!

When people come to church they must leave with a fire set in their hearts. Passion must be kindled and God presented as the prize. Let us stop prioritizing the "wrong things"; working in the house of God, giving tithes and offerings, growing large denominations and beautifying our buildings. I believe this is what God meant when He was saying they had left the weightier things and focused on things that do not matter. Let us not become caught in the same trap. I would like every church minister, worker or general overseer to prayerfully meditate over our church services. When people leave church on service days, what exactly do they leave with? What impressions do we create? What passion do we ignite in their hearts? If we sincerely ask these questions I believe our response will help trigger change.

Mathew 23:23
"Woe to you, teachers of the law and Pharisees, you hypocrites! You give a tenth of your spices--mint, dill and cumin. But you have neglected the more important matters of the law--justice, mercy and faithfulness. You

should have practiced the latter, without neglecting the former." KJV

It is impressed strongly on my heart that what God desires with structures and organization around our churches; our organizations, denominations, proliferations and growth in the cities are not to sell a "needy" gospel but to enable the church become a family of believers indeed. It is to make it easier for us to physically meet each other's emotional, physical, financial and material needs. These are not supposed to be the central theme of our prayer meetings. Our giving and tithing should take care of the financial needs of those who are poor amongst us. Our Pastors are to meet the emotional needs of those who are feeble or downcast by pointing them to God through godly counsel. The sickness in our body should be healed as we fellowship and lay hands. These however cannot become the "gospel" which we preach because this "gospel" produces dead, passionless and immature Christians.

We need the church to once again be filled with people crying just for the Father. Our focus must return to personal, sincere experiences with God.

Let me ask you dear reader, when last were you in a church service where you didn't feel held back or restricted. When last were you in a service where your eyes welled up in tears as the preacher pointed you back to God? When last were you in a church service where it wasn't just about what God can do for you or how many demons, devils or witches need to be "killed"? When last did you come into church and all you did was worship the King? When last did you come to church and after the service, you went home to lock yourself up crying for more of God? I dare say just few of us have had such experiences in recent times.

Dear church worker, there is a place in God where you don't need to be feeling like serving Him is so burdensome. Serving God can be so filled with passion, love, peace and liberty. You can do what you do in your denomination without feeling as if it were a chore or burden. You can give without a grudge. You can serve with passion! I wish you would wherever you are fall on your face and cry for God alone.

We have become clones of our senior pastors and general overseers. Is it not funny that the man you are trying to copy and look like is being himself while you are enslaved by trying to be someone else? The whole world is groaning for you to manifest your uniqueness and originality which God Himself put in you for a reason. Yet you are stuck in a cycle of imitation. A wise man said imitation is the worst form of flattery.

See how Myles Munroe put it:
"Don't be a pigeon if you were born to be an eagle. Experience God's altitude for your life."
"You must decide if you are going to rob the world or bless it with the rich, valuable, potent, untapped resources locked away within

you."

"A true leader does not measure his success by comparing himself to others but by evaluating how he is fulfilling his own purpose and vision."

These words from this man of God are so true today as they were the day he spoke them. We need to begin to celebrate our uniqueness in God.

Organized religion gives the impression that if you are not like the man who leads you, you are not correct. I have been in meetings where one denomination says "we cannot be like so and so of another denomination because they are not our father" Honestly dear church leader who are we supposed to be looking like? You or God? We have so many people who walk, talk, dress, preach, sing, marry, and even attempt to live their everyday lives like their general overseers and therefore the pulpit has become powerless and a place for indoctrination. The fear is that we are now transferring this same emptiness of religion to the pews.

A man wakes up one day and puts gel on his hair because obviously, that's what he likes. Then every pastor under him goes and does likewise. We are told that when the senior pastor kneels during worship we all who are "under him" must kneel also, because we do not know what he saw that he knelt down. So now we have religious activity during worship. The man preaching kneels and we all kneel "because we do not know what he saw..." How sad that we would make this an issue in church. When one refuses to kneel, he is told he has no spiritual home training or better still he has no respect for God's anointed. What hurts the most in this "ritual" is the fact that most of these people (church leaders/senior pastors) have made a routine out of it. They just kneel because they must (for whatever reason known to them) not because they saw God walk into the room. So now, everyone in the church is kneeling religiously without any true sense of purpose. Are we surprised that our worship is empty of life? It is all music and no Spirit... nothing! Religious activity can never birth true passion for God in the heart of a believer. Never!

I ask simply, who are we to see when we worship; The senior pastor or God?
Honestly if our pastors will spend more time teaching the people how to see God in worship, we would need no one to tell us to kneel when worship starts. Obviously, our senses would have been trained to discern; we would then be able to see what supposedly the senior pastor sees.

Imagine a man walks into church, sees people kneeling with their eyes closed and he asks what is happening? The response will be "nothing really, our senior pastor knelt down so we all had to kneel in respect". The man too then joins the kneeling group so he is not the odd one out. I fear that the world mocks us; they wonder how we could be so bent on doing things for doing sake without any true purpose. Most believers especially church workers do things in church without ever knowing why. They attend meetings without knowing why, they serve without knowing why, and they give offerings without knowing why. Some are now even getting married without knowing why!

Am I saying we should not emulate our pastors and leaders over us? No sir! Paul dealt with something like this in 1 Corinthians 11. Let us look at this verse in various translations:

1 Corinthians 11:1
"Be ye followers of me, even as I also am of Christ." KJV
"PATTERN YOURSELVES after me [follow my example], as I imitate and follow Christ (the Messiah)." AMP
"So take me for your example, even as I take Christ for mine" BBE
"Be imitators of me, as I am of Christ" ESV
"Follow my example, as I follow the example of Christ" NIV

This verse does not stand alone in isolation. There was some discourse in chapter ten that led up to this. In fact, Paul says in the last verses of chapter ten *"So whether you eat or drink or whatever you do, do it all for the glory of God. Do not cause anyone to stumble, whether Jews, Greeks or the church of God— even as I try to please everyone in every way. For I am not seeking my own good but the good of many, so that they may be saved" 1Cor 10:31-33*

So, based on the above, follow my example. That was the thought behind the first verse of chapter 11. He then goes further in verse two to provide other traditions he expected them to follow.

That verse had nothing with becoming a clone or being indoctrinated. He wanted them to understand that Christ had a demand on his life, he was following Christ to ensure he meets that demand, and he encouraged those following him to do so with that understanding.

There is a crisis in Christendom and I perceive that with this dissatisfaction that so many in the body are feeling, God is calling us to return to genuine Christianity. He is pointing the way out of religion and calling us again to a passionate pursuit of His face.

A friend and brother of mine shared a dream he had with me. In that dream it seems God had called him out of our denomination to start another work. He was looking at the new church building and explaining to someone his reasons for leaving and said "religion had held me bound for 15 years". Beloved imagine the weight this my brother was feeling for him to be expressing it even in his dream. We cannot be satisfied anymore with doctrines we want passion! True heartfelt passion!

Moses said please Lord... Show me your glory! It seems to me he had come to a place where nothing else would satisfy. Now, if Moses who the Lord spoke to face to face cried "show me your glory", the question becomes what was he seeing when God spoke to Him that he still yearned for His glory? Beloved there are dimensions in God and hunger is the currency for spiritual progress in the realm of the spirit. Oh God! Please bring your church to the place of genuine hunger for You in this season. We are tired of religion.

Dear church pastor, bishop, leader and general overseer, I challenge you to call a meeting with your church workers and ask them to speak honestly and openly with you. You would discover the lack of fulfilment, dis-satisfaction and discontent that fills their hearts. Some have been around you and your denomination for maybe 30 years and have never encountered God for themselves. They are sick of giving and not receiving, fed up with some of the prayers you and the church pray, and are desperately looking for something deeper. They have been doing the same things for years and we all know these things are not working. Yet most of us are afraid to point it out. The prayers are not working sir. The people you delivered last week are here again. Those whom demons flew out from (and they ended up breaking half the chairs in church) are here again this week. We are hurt, broken, disappointed, lonely, sick, unemployed and on and on… These things we have been doing are not working. Don't you think we should change the emphasis?

There are more questions in the heart of Christians than answers and we cannot continue to pretend that these questions do not exist or that they have been answered. We must confront the issues being raised in the hearts of men and trust God to bring us to the place of true fulfilment.

The people are worried, pastors themselves are worried but no one dare speak up. We all stay put only because we cannot think of a "better" place to go. Many think of changing denominations but when you look on the other side, they too have their problems so one better stays where he is. After all, "the devil you know is better than the angel you don't." Plus, if we all leave, who would bring the needed change? The solution is not to abandon the church but for us all to work together to get it right.

Oh, tears fill my eyes as I read the stories of the apostles and men who not too long ago walked the face of the earth. Their passion for God and His work makes what we do in present day seem like child's play.

Mark 7:13 –
"Making the word of God of none effect through your tradition, which ye have delivered: and many such like things do ye" KJV

Acts 4:33
"And with great power the apostles gave witness of the resurrection of Jesus: and great grace was upon them all" Oh, that men in my generation will push beyond rituals, dead church services, traditions and other limitation in organized religion and press into God.

God stir our hearts for you and you alone today!

WASTED EXISTENCE

*The greatest tragedy in life is not death
but a life without purpose*
— Myles Munroe

There is nothing worse than being alive and not knowing why
— Myles Munroe.

This then is the purpose of life: to see God
— Roy and Revel Hession

In the quietness of my soul, deeply brooding over all that is happening around us in Christendom, I fear that we have done little to create a lasting impression in the hearts of men. What exactly will our communities, villages, cities, towns, countries and continents remember about the church? What picture have we put in the hearts of the everyday man or woman who interacts with the local church? If we would carefully attempt to answer this question, I fear we might painfully realize that ours in this generation has been but a wasted existence.

A wise man said *"This is life more abundant – the life of power! The real life of satisfaction. The life of knowing that your living has not been in vain. Surely it is worth every sacrifice to know that we have followed in the steps of the Son of God".*

Paul the Apostle gave us the revelations of grace and the finished works of Christ, King James gave us the bible and the opportunity to put God's Word in the hands of millions of people, Wesley and the Methodist church gave us a new move of the Spirit and revival, Charles H. Spurgeon revolutionized the church in England opening the doors to anyone who wanted to come. What exactly have we prepared and given for the next generation to build on? With all our "noise" and activity, we have done little to build on the great works those of them who went ahead of us. A wise man said "if what you did yesterday continues to look great, then it means you have done nothing today". There is a constant and consistent reference to the "days of old" so it tells me we have done nothing today. Our revivals of today pale in comparism to the revivals of old. Our sacrifices today seem like child's play when put side by side with those who were not careful even at the expense of their lives. In the Nigerian church, we have replaced brother and sister with daddy and mummy, such that church leaders now arrogate unnecessary respect and power to themselves yet we have no results when compared to those who were simply brothers and sisters or didn't even bother to add titles to their names.

I fear that we might have "lived" longer but ours has been a wasted existence. I wish the church would stop all the activity and cry to God to begin with us again. We have driven the Holy Spirit out of our churches with our legalistic approach. Laws and doctrines have taken over our services such that our poise betrays us; we say with our mouth that we need the Holy Spirit but our decisions, actions and results are void of His presence. His influence cannot be felt or seen in the way our leaders act or talk. His nature cannot be seen in what drives us. Our passions, appetites and ambitions betray our complete lack of trust, dependency and strength in the Holy Spirit. Most of what goes on in our denominations have been achieved by the arm of flesh just that we have laced it with a little spirituality so it looks like it is God who wrought it.

I would like to use a scripture that blessed me to emphasize this point here.

Gen 5:21-24
"And Enoch lived sixty and five years, and begat Methuselah: And Enoch walked with God after he begat Methuselah three hundred years and begat sons and daughters: And all the days of Enoch were three hundred and sixty five years: And Enoch walked with God: and he was not; for God took him"

I implore you dear reader to pause here and please go back to read Genesis 5 from verse 1 which begins with "This is the book of generations of Adam..." It would help give you a better understanding as I attempt to use this to explain what God put in my spirit.

As we read the chapter in question, we notice how beginning with Adam, scriptures mention how long the individual lived, and then how many children they had, and then when they died. This is the pattern in this genealogy until we come to verse 21 where Enoch is introduced. Suddenly the pattern changes;

where we would normally see how long the man lived, how many children he had and when he died, we now see a punctuation "Enoch walked with God..." Notice that immediately after this wonderful punctuation in history, we go back to the drab status quo of seeming meaningless existence with the others mentioned after Enoch.

What intrigues me the most about this line of history is the fact that all the people before and after Enoch lived almost twice the amount of years (or more) he did, but none had the same level of impact or testimony with God. The church has got to realize that life is not in quantity but in quality. It is not how long we have been that matters but in the quality of our existence. I believe this is what God was trying to show us with this chapter of scriptures. It is not in how many countries your church can be found. Neither is it in how large your congregations are or how many branches you have in the continents of the world. It is in the value you have created and the lives you have brought face to face with Jesus. "Enoch walked with God..." It seems God wants us to see that it is possible to break the status quo and do what is expected even though everyone else might be comfortable with the "abnormal". What happened to Enoch that led him to decide to take a different path from all his fathers, brothers and sisters before him? I am hoping that this book will cause same to happen to us in this generation.

I personally learnt a few things about life from this portion of scripture.

#1 Life is a test
Beloved child of God reading this book today, life is a test! And like every test, it demands that we prepare if not we would end up as failures. I fear that organized religion has neglected the place of preparation hence the increase in the amount of moral failures amongst church leaders. Anyone can become a pastor in certain denominations these days. All you need do is join the church, become a church worker, do all that is asked of you and then, bam! Few months later you are standing the pulpit dishing out "death" to the pew. So, we have people who have never encountered God on a personal level, who have had no dealings with God concerning the flaws in their lives and are still in a continuous battle with carnality, standing to lead other men. The sad thing about this is, what kind of children do you expect this kind of men to produce? We have men in the pulpit who got there only because they were able to generate huge returns from their place of assignment for the headquarter church. Now they continue to milk people so "greasing of the palms" of those above can continue. This in the long run, helps to generate further "juicy" positions in the pulpit. What kind of church do you expect such men to produce?

Let us teach our people what I call "The Law of Life". This law simply says "everything will produce after its own kind". Unprepared men leading the church have led us deeper and deeper into religion. Every man called into ministry must have had a point in his or her life when God encountered such a one. There must be some day they can refer to as the day God spoke clearly concerning His assignment for their lives. Sadly, we do not emphasize this anymore. We emphasize things like loyalty to the denomination, amount of tithe paid, and other things that make doing God's assignment look like some CEO position in a business or political office in a nation.

Therefore, there is now politics in the church. Positions are given based on how much you can send upwards. People are promoted based on how many branches they can open and no one is looking at the inner lives of the men who we are handing over God's people to. No wonder failure is on the rise. We claim to be celebrating successes but I can tell you God is saying we are failing. A wise man of God said "In ministry, training must precede positioning otherwise there will be irreparable damage" The work of the ministry involves the handling of the lives of men. To put this in the hands of unprepared men is a gamble too expensive because of the irreparable damage it can cause. Yet we continue to take this chance because we must expand, grow our denominations and meet targets we set for ourselves.

Life is a test and God expects us to prepare accordingly. Our inability to prepare properly cannot be traced back to God for He has ensured we have all we need in His Word to point us in the right direction. If we then fail the test of life as a church, God will hold us accountable.

We do not encourage preparation, separation and personal dealings with God anymore because the Christian leaders believe we can do all we do without help from the Holy Spirit. We choose leaders without praying, we ordain pastors based on if they are from the same tribe or community as our general overseers or bishops, we celebrate those whom we believe are "loyal" and bring them before God to then approve. We now have a show where we seem to want God to approve a man He did not choose. Can this really be done? No sir! We choose them, we approve them but God just stands aside. There is a public display like it is God that has approved but in the spirit realm flesh has just been glorified. Little wonder no power continues to beget no power. Our pulpits are void of the life of the Holy Spirit. God cannot use unprepared men to showcase His power.

A young believer watching a senior pastor in a certain denomination speak cringed as he wondered if the man was even born again. He couldn't hold back as he spoke to another believer sitting by "I would never be a minister in this denomination". How can a so-called church leader or senior pastor be speaking like this? I tell you how, religion got him to where he is today. We chose him and tried to "force" God to approve him alas God will never put His seal on what He has not approved. He will never sponsor what He didn't initiate. Hence, we have carnal unregenerate men leading God's people. Most heart wrenching about this picture is the fact that in organized religion, we see nothing wrong with this. We have become so comfortable that we are even in a hurry to get more men like this in positions of ministry.

The kind of demands we place on people in organized religion makes the cry of Jesus in Mathew 11:28-30 seem like a lie!

"Come unto me all ye that labour and are heavy laden, and I will give you rest. Take my yoke upon you, and learn of me; for I am meek and lowly in heart: and ye shall find rest for your souls. For my yoke is easy and my burden is light"

Organized religion is putting burdens and yokes upon God's people that makes the scripture above untenable. There is no rest for the souls of men within the walls of our denominations anymore because those who should point them to the savior are the ones now demanding worship and honour from them. One is forced to ask; if men are demanding so much honor, what then is left for Jesus who gave His life for us? Jesus said "I am meek and lowly in heart…" This I dare say can no longer be said of our so-called pastors, bishops and general overseers in the organized religion we call Christianity in my generation. "Big" or "senior" pastors as they are called can no longer be invited to small churches. The protocol involved will make us weep. The bottle necks would make one feel like he is literally trying to make something impossible possible. Men could literally get suspended or removed from certain ministry offices for daring or attempting to invite a man above them in church hierarchy. How dare you invite the senior man of God? Who are you to invite him? Did you come and tell me first? How many members do you have that you want him to come and minister? How much honorarium can you afford? These and many more are the kind of questions one will encounter if an attempt was made to invite a senior pastor to a small church. This is the sad and sorry state of ministry in my generation. The anointing on certain men can only flow in large auditoriums and big churches. Especially those where the honorarium package will be "befitting".

For some pastors, our anointing can only work in an atmosphere where there is air-conditioning and the expectation of fat offerings. Hence, we no longer go to small churches where we would get "nothing". The spirit of prophecy would naturally drop on us only when we are in the "right kind" of church. So, we have churches in the same denomination; one almost looks like a pig sty with nothing happening there in terms of revival while the other seems to be a palace with all the so-called move of God thriving there. Same church family, same denomination, same city. When everybody decides to go to the bigger church, they say the man in the smaller church has no anointing hence he can't grow the church. Sir, since we are in the same work, and you have the anointing, please go to the smaller church for a few months and grow the church. However, this never happens!

Life is a test and we must be committed to returning to proper preparation so that we can avoid failure otherwise ours will be described as a wasted existence.

God is constantly seeking men like Enoch who in a generation will arise and challenge the status quo; I would rather die than live for many years without any relevance with and for God. Let's get out of our comfort zones and really do ministry. I fear that so many of us have gotten too comfortable that we are no longer hearing the call of God to the place of preparation lest we faint in the day of adversary.

Life is a test!

#2 Life is a trust

2 Corinthians 5:10
"For we must all appear before the judgment seat of Christ; that everyone may receive the things done is his body according to that he hath done, whether it be good or bad"

At some point, we all are going to stand before Christ who is the head of the church and we would give account of all we have done here (in this world) whether good or bad. Paul reminds us that as stewards we are expected to be faithful but sadly my generation does not realize that life is a trust. The one who gave the opportunity will one day come to ask "what did you do with it?" I allowed you the priviledge to gather millions of men but how did you help their lives? Too many so-called church gatherings are a complete waste of time. Forgive me for sounding like this but this is the hard truth.

Like I said at the beginning of this book, I do not speak as one who has attained. Concerning these issues I have raised here, I confront myself with same daily. If indeed I say I have contacted God I too must produce results flowing from that encounter. This book is to provoke the church in my generation to desire something deeper than what we are currently experiencing.

Our focus is on tithes, offerings and other "selfish" things. One cannot remember when he attended a meeting and there was a push to seek God for more of Himself. The focus has so shifted that one can easily predict what he would hear in church soon as the preacher begins his sermon. The punch lines and endings are all the same. Most times we end by telling people to come sow seeds for twenty-four-hour miracles. We have developed theology around numbers (supported by very powerful testimonies of those whom it worked for either by hook or crook) to syphon more money from people. Beloved, life is a trust and we all will stand before the head of the church to give account.

If this will dawn on us in this generation, we would be careful how we lead and how we follow. Paul says from the passage we mentioned above, that our deeds and motives will be judged; the bad which is obvious and the good if it was good enough.

So many church leaders will say "my denomination is doing or has done this and that for the people I am leading" but God will ask if the good you say you have done was good enough. Compared to the resources at your disposal, when put side by side with the platform God gave, can you say you have done noble? The response will have nothing to do with the size of our auditoriums, bank accounts, nations we have visited or how many branches we successfully opened. Alas it will be in the quality of lives sitting in our pews.

The life you have is not your own. The ministry you are leading or serving in is not your own either. He gave you an opportunity and the question is, have you abused or maximized this opportunity?

The church is His body. I feel we have forgotten this in my generation, so we trivialize the souls of men. We think as long as we preach one or two sermons on salvation and hell then we have done enough. There are abuses of the Christian faith so glaring to the world around us and it bothers me that those of us on the inside are pretending not to see it. I fear that God will remind us *"my name has been profaned amongst the heathen because of you"*. See *Ezekiel 36:20-23. The way we are carrying on invariably has contributed to people of the world refusing to join us. In many families, passionate Christians have become objects of scorn because they are seen to be pouring their lives into something that seems not to be working.*

I feel the need to drive this home; we would give account for the sheep in our care. As a preacher myself, I do not cease to ask God to help me so I do not give out dead sermons that produce no life in the people who I lead. The burden of leadership sometimes is so immense that I cry to God for help. I do not want to "frustrate" those whom God has put in my hands. I earnestly long to see the Word of God producing results in the lives of those whom I lead and for this I hold unto God with the sincere yearnings of my soul. And when I speak about results, my focus is not on brand new cars, houses or material things but hunger and passion for God and His work; the manifestation of a true child of God. Walking and living in the supernatural.

One day I too will stand to give account. There are no excuses beloved child of God. When we stand before the judgment seat of Christ all the exaggerations on the pulpit just so the message would sound better will be judged. All the manipulations so you could win favour or get an item off that sheep whom God sent to you would be judged. It is either we pleased Him or we did not. I dare not even begin to speak about the consequences, for some of you know a lot more than myself in that regard. It is very easy to make excuses for the religious things we do in our denominations especially when we are getting results. It is easy to justify the "wrong" as long as we have some evidence that seemingly shows God's approval but one day we would stand face to face with Him who gave His life for the church and I fear He would ask us "Is this the church I died for?" A wise man said "God's way of judging a man as successful is not based on works or results. It is based on faithfulness. No matter how fruitful you are, if you are not faithful, you are not successful"

I do not believe Christ died so we could arrive at where we are now in Christendom. There is so much more we are to be reaping/enjoying from His sacrifice and yet we cannot experience them because we have chosen to swim in the murky waters of religion. There are so many benefits of the finished works of Christ but we focus only on the material and hence have little of supernatural experiences.

Let us take it further and "hit the nail on the head".

Where has freedom of worship gone? There is this air of restriction and limitation in our denominations. It is so tangible that when you walk into certain so called church services you can almost touch it. It is like the people are in chains; feeling like they must do something to be accepted by God, or have to possess a certain feeling or attribute of character to be blessed by God.

"I do not frustrate the grace of God: for if righteousness comes by the law, then Christ is dead in vain" Gal 2:21

Legalism and traditions "handcuff" our services and grace seems only fit to stand at the door. I fear that even if the Holy Spirit wanted to move in our services, we would not have room for Him. In so many denominations, we have patterns and traditions that have stylishly shut out the spontaneity of the Holy Spirit. Sometimes I am sitting in a service and wondering, where is God in all of this? Even if He wanted to show up, we would not allow Him. Our order of service and program of events would not allow the Holy Spirit. He who should be the essence/center of the service would seem as an interruption to most.

No wonder we have very little demonstration of the genuine power of God in my generation.

Beloved Christian community, we would give account one day. We have made God so difficult to reach that the average man sitting in our pews has his head bent in self-condemnation. We are pushing men away from God instead of encouraging them to run to Him. Little wonder there is so much pretense in church.

Church workers with no passion or prayer life continue doing what they do for fear of being found out. So, we put up a face, follow the rules and traditions just to feel like part of the body. Church leaders will never notice because we are engrossed in our hair being covered and gathering for conferences and camp meetings that we hardly notice the air of inner conflict in the lives of our people. What happened to *"where the Spirit of the Lord is there is liberty"*? 2 Corinthians 3:17.

What some of us experience in church is very far from liberty!

Life is a trust and one day... The head of the Church will ask "Your time spent on earth what did it amount to?" I can only focus on what my answer will be. What will yours be?

#3 Life is short

Job 14:1&5

"Man that is born of a woman is of few days and full of trouble"

"Seeing that his days are determined, the number of his months are with thee, thou has appointed his bounds that he cannot cross"

I remember watching a message Myles Munroe preached at the Azusa camp meeting (or revival) in 1990. He was probably only in his early twenties and he said "God has given me a huge assignment but I don't have enough time" This man of God lived to be over sixty years old. All through his life delivering profound truths to the body of Christ and making tremendous impact not only in Christendom but in governments of the world. He was a solid example of bringing the King's kingdom influence on earth. When I heard him speak those words in that message, it opened to me one of the reasons for his tremendous success; he understood that life was short and one day he would have to go home. He prepared for his exit with every work he did in ministry. This was a man who understood the dynamics of life and maximized it. He continues to inspire me in death even as he did in life.

There is so much God desires to do in this realm and with this generation. There is a cry in the heavens for sons of God to arise and do the bidding of the Father. I hear groans in the heavens as God aches for a man or woman to arise out of the lethargy of present day Christianity and advance the purposes of Elohim in this generation. Alas... Christians in this generation forget that the Master calls for lives that will be lived accurately and in alignment with the agenda of the Father.

For the Christian to be useful to God's agenda, we must live in the constant realization of the shortness of life and the inevitability of eternity but the average Christian is encumbered. The cares of life our biggest burden driving us farther and farther from genuine spiritual reality. What to eat, what to wear, where to live and bills to pay have become a millstone hung on the soul of the average believer! After all said and done, what will heaven credit to our accounts when our time here is called? A wise man said, "may you have more done than said".

I fear that with the way we are carrying on in Christendom, we have completely forgotten that we have a huge mandate from God but we have very little time. We have become busier than normal but I fear we have caused a sharp deviation from God's original intention for the church. Our outlook suggests that we believe we have more than enough time hence we can afford to keep the essence of our calling waiting while we engage in frivolities and "noise making". Like a popular movie title, we are "busy but guilty".

In Exodus, God calls Moses and gives him a pattern for His tabernacle. He tells him exactly how he should build the meeting place (including all the items to be placed therein) because that's where He (God) wants to dwell. God specifically mentions to Moses the need for him to stick to what he had been shown.

Exodus 25:40 *"Study the design you were given on the mountain and make everything accordingly."* MSG

If Moses had chosen to build outside of the pattern of God, God would not have stopped him but guaranteed, God will never have come to dwell there. He would have had all the resources from God at his disposal, expended them on the wrong pattern and "fooled" men that he was in the center of God's will concerning the tabernacle. Only Moses and God would have known the whole truth of the matter at hand.

The church in my generation has the same (if not more) resources as Moses did; Moses had Bezaleel and Aholiab the skilled and spirit filled workers chosen specifically for the task (See Exodus 31:1-11) just as we have numerous workers in our various denominations. Peradventure Moses decided to go his own way, he would have ended up abusing the resources provided for him. Many church workers are disenchanted and are leaving our organized and structured denominations because we are constantly using them inappropriately. This abuse has got to stop! Our assignment is to build according to the pattern. So many things we are doing today have no basis when compared to what God has showed us in His Word. He warned Moses "study the design and ensure you build according to what I showed you on the mountain". I do agree that many men have said "God spoke to them" but if we would be honest, only the man himself knows the voice he heard. God might have spoken and the man chose his own interpretation. Only God knows!

Wrong patterns lead to excessive burdens and excessive burdens always produce frustration. There is no excitement amongst church workers any more. People are just doing what they do in their denominations to fulfil all righteousness but over 90% are disenchanted. If we would allow them to be sincere then we would hear their hearts.

The church of God in my generation seems to be building various patterns of Christianity and those watching from outside are confused as to what we really represent. We are in a mad rush for structures, bigger churches, and all manner of traditions but the core design given by God has been deviated from. The danger with this is, we waste the short time we have here building strange patterns and end up excluding God from our meetings. On the outside, it all looks like God is involved because there are so many beautiful sanctuary buildings, a million branches here and there, millions of members across the globe but alas it has been a wasted existence. We have deviated from the pattern.

Beloved, I weep sometimes when I hear some pastors speaking. You hear things like "this is how we have been doing it" or "our bishop said this is the way it must be done if we don't do it like this then we don't belong to this denomination" We are raising clones of denominational doctrines but few men who have really encountered God. We are wasting our energies organizing programs and meetings, but we are generating so little results. Does it not bother you dear reader that in our cities and villages in Nigeria, church signboards fill the streets. Churches are on a steady increase in numbers but we do not see a commensurate influence on the fabric of our society. Evil, sin and immorality continues to thrive, yet we gather in large numbers in our church auditoriums. The apostles and disciples of old by their way of life conquered the great empire of Rome and brought her to her knees before the Holy and Righteous one – Jehovah. Does it not trouble you dear reader that our denominations have grown bigger but our results have remained so small? Are questions not raised in your heart when hundreds of thousands or millions gather in a crusade or special program but only five or ten eventually come out to share testimonies? Are you not tired dear reader of talk and no proofs? We seem to have made the God shown us in the bible into a liar. The Word of God seems not to work in the face of real situations, our prayers seem to go unanswered even when we fast for 21, 100, and 400 days, and our lives seem not to be producing the same results when compared with those before us who received the same Holy Spirit we claim to have received. Is it not possible that we are in "tabernacles" that have not followed the design shown by God? God cannot come where deviations have become accepted as the norm.

The proliferation of so called bible believing churches is on a steady increase in Nigeria. All you need to do on Sunday is walk around your street and it will shock you the number of churches you would see. The question then becomes how come we are not seeing the express glory of God manifested and covering this country?

We have fuller churches, more organized structures and management but very little results. Why? Because it is all organized religion! We are celebrating progress yet God's heart bleeds because we have so short a time and yet we are wasting our existence.

I remember I was at a meeting and we were expecting the man of God who was to minister. A "big" and popular man of God. The place was packed full; we were under the scorching sun sweating profusely and I began to see men pushing and fussing just to get in. Some were being brought in on stretchers, some on wheel chairs, some incapacitated all looking for help from our God. I felt pain welling up in my heart as the meeting came to a close because all these people went back the same way they came. Not one miracle or move of God's Spirit happened in the time we were there. After the long wait, you could now find people hobbling (because they were leaving with their sicknesses and diseases) back into their vehicles, struggling under the scorching sun to go back where they came from. Then I stood there wondering and discomfited inside. Is this God's will for His church? We spent over four hours in that place waiting for the man of God and yet left dissatisfied. Is this how God planned it? When I look at the bible I see differently and it "damages" me… The dissatisfaction I feel inside threatens to rip me apart. Like Isaiah I seem to be crying "I am undone! I am undone!!"

I weep because this is not the pattern, God's original design includes the manifestation of His power when we gather. But alas, if we would be sincere with ourselves, most of our gatherings are usually a waste of time. People make tremendous sacrifices to gather wherever we ask them to and at the end, there is nothing tangible to point to as a result of the meeting.

Where two or three are gathered in His name there He is in the midst of them. Christ is the pattern that God has given to us and if we check His own life we see the same situation like I described above howbeit but with different results; He healed them ALL.

The major reason we have such mega gatherings but so little results is because we have forgotten life is short and have spent time building organizations and structures while the main work of God is suffering. The saddest part of that my story is that, the church leaders on the day and so many others were so happy the man of God came at all; nothing else mattered. I wondered if I was abnormal to be feeling the way I felt deep down. How can we have so little time to spend on earth and yet be so comfortable with mediocrity and a complete lack of results? We celebrate one or two empty wheel chairs, few miracles and we become comfortable. Beloved that is not the pattern!

It is time to fall on our face and cry... oh God so much to do but so little time to do it. Pour upon us fire that we might fulfill your assignment and build according to the pattern again. Father increase our influence in the world. May nations, kings and kingdoms come to the church for guidance, solutions and direction!

These three things I shared with you, were impressed on my heart as I read that scripture about Enoch in the book of Genesis. Life is a test, trust and it is short. Because life is all these things, ultimately, life can be wasted. The minute one refuses to prepare, position and propel per the pattern, surely, we would be staring at a wasted existence.

It seems to me that the Holy Spirit wants us to look at the genealogy of the last Adam who is Jesus Christ. He has had many sons and daughters and from time to time you will see a punctuation in the family tree like that of Enoch where one son or daughter will walk with God and cause the church to go back to her original purpose. At these points in history we would normally recognize this as a revival and there have been so many we can refer to that have given direction, gust and purpose to the church. However, I fear that my generation seem to be

Methuselah on the family tree; we have existed for so long yet we have so little results when compared to the Enochs before us. Why is this? Is the glory of the latter not supposed to be greater than the former?

We keep living, growing, expanding, enlarging, organizing and developing. We are increasing in years but have no markers to refer to. No tangible experience to point to the fact that we have indeed walked with God. If Enoch walked with God and God took him, what then has been the result of the church in my generation seemingly walking with God?

We have been deceived because this Methuselah has lived for so long and so we think we can continue with business as usual because there is still much time to live. Organized religion will continue to thrive, boom and even get little results but authentic Christianity is on a steady decline. I ask fellow soldier of the cross, which would you rather have?

May we not weep when we stand before the Master. May His Words not pierce through our hearts as a double-edged sword as we realize that though we lived long, we did not live well. Ours was but a wasted existence.

We dare not wait till that wonderful day soon to be upon us. We must fall on our faces and cry to God to kill religion and religious activity before it kills us. We must determine to seek God's face in prayer until our church leaders realize that we are going the wrong way. We must pray, pray and pray again until the abuse within our denominations come to an end. After all, what else can we do but call upon Him who is head of the church to help His body?

God please help your church in my generation! We want to build according to the pattern again.

Please Lord, help your church.

The Supernatural Generation

When a man who crept along for years in conventional Christianity suddenly zooms into spiritual alertness, becomes aggressive in the battle of the Lord, and has a quenchless zeal for the lost, there is a reason for it.
(But we are so subnormal these days that the normal New Testament experience seems abnormal).
— Leonard Ravenhill

The two prerequisites to successful living are vision and passion, both of which are born in and maintained by prayer.
— Leonard Ravenhill

Before we build on the thoughts God will have us ruminate on here, let us read a portion of scripture to give shape (or form) in our minds as we read on.

Joel 2:2-11
It is a day of darkness and gloom, a day of thick clouds and deep blackness. Suddenly, like dawn spreading across the mountains, a great and mighty army appears. Nothing like it has been seen before or will ever be seen again. Fire burns in front of them, and flames follow after them. Ahead of them the land lies as beautiful as the Garden of Eden. Behind them is nothing but desolation; not one thing escapes.

They look like horses; they charge forward like warhorses. Look at them as they leap along the mountaintops. Listen to the noise they make—like the rumbling of chariots, like the roar of fire sweeping across a field of stubble, or like a mighty army moving into battle.

Fear grips all the people; every face grows pale with terror. The attackers march like warriors and scale city walls like soldiers. Straight forward they march, never breaking rank. They never jostle each other; each moves in exactly the right position. They break through defenses without missing a step. They swarm over the city and run along its walls. They enter all the houses, climbing like thieves through the windows. The earth quakes as they advance, and the heavens tremble. The sun and moon grow dark, and the stars no longer shine. The Lord is at the head of the column. He leads them with a shout. This is his mighty army, and they follow his orders. The day of the Lord is an awesome, terrible thing. Who can possibly survive?"

I am tired of our generation being called "The Powerless Generation". We have structures, rules and traditions but we have not been able to bring God's power to bear when faced with real life situations. It seems like we are the generation always looking at years past to find inspiration because there seems to be nothing today or ahead to give us hope. Sickness, disease, starvation, perversion, fornication and all manner of ungodliness stir us in the face but we seem powerless to bring change. With pain in my heart I write this today; I am tired of us being described as the powerless generation. It is time for us to become what God intended – The Supernatural Generation.

The face of Christianity as we know it today will gradually begin to change in no distant time. There are signs in the spirit realm pointing to a shift (many have become grossly dissatisfied with what has been happening) and very soon it will no longer be business as usual. Denominations that do not align with the happenings in the realm of the spirit might have nothing left during and after this shift.

Situations are fast rising that will challenge the very core of our beliefs. Diseases and sicknesses, epidemics and viruses, tsunamis, hurricanes and natural disasters are all on the increase. What this suggests is, men who have genuine solutions to all these challenges will become essential commodities for governments and nations of the world. Men who possess answers to "difficult" questions will become indispensable.

Peoples from every tribe, tongue and creed in nations of the world are fast realizing that the structures that have been built by their governments and economies overtime; when viewed in the context of what could possibly go wrong, will not be sufficient for disaster management and recovery if the adverse circumstances we have been experiencing were to be a notch greater than what we have experienced so far.

The world is slowly acknowledging that science, medicine and medical doctors are increasingly becoming overwhelmed with the diseases requiring vaccines and cures. It is fearfully obvious that if an epidemic were to breakout in Nigeria for instance, men, women and children would die like flies before any reasonable help or relief could be proffered. The world; more so Africa and Nigeria are grossly unprepared for what the devil seems to be packaging for us in this generation. Therefore, God who knows the end of a thing even from the beginning; our God who nothing can take unawares has begun to train and prepare a new set of people to provide answers to these questions when the time comes.

There are generals being raised in the secret. A breed of seekers and inquirers who want nothing but to ascend the mysterious heights of spirituality such that there are so conscious of God and nothing else matters. There is a supernatural generation rising and even before the devil began to plan his next attack, God had already described them in Joel chapter 2. A generation of believers who have refused to be pegged down by religion. A set of people who have soaked in the Word and realize there is more to God than what we are currently experiencing in our denominations. A group of men and women who are ready to prove the Word of God in the circumstances and situations of life. Men and women of evidence, proofs and results. Men and women of the supernatural.

I know this has begun to happen because I hear messages being preached on certain pulpits in Nigeria. At some point I was thinking "I am all alone on this journey", been misunderstood and spoken about/against. But in recent times, God has encouraged my heart like He did the prophet. "I have reserved for myself 7,000 who have not bowed the knee to Baal" 1 Kings 19:18. I listen to some preachers (young and old) in Nigeria; some very close and known to me in a one-on-one relationship and others I just happen to know from a distance; their messages have been a source of inspiration and joy though we have never met. For these preachers I speak about, their passion, commitment and zeal for God's work in these end times breeds confidence in my heart. I would have loved to name names but that is not the purpose of this book.

These men I speak of belong to different denominations but somehow their message seem to align with what God has lit in my own heart. It tells me, God indeed is already raising an end time army.

I seem to always find a way to come back to this end time army in my books because God spoke specifically to me about this years ago as He was dealing with me as regards ministry. I am confident more than ever that we would see this army rise in Nigeria and Africa in no distant time.

If those that listen will now begin to take what is being said seriously and engage God in the place of prayer, then Africa and Nigeria can be prepared to experience the remnant who have refused to bow to religion and religious activity. The supernatural generation is already rising!

My challenge to you dear reader is, would you be part of this supernatural generation or are you comfortable with what we have now that we call Christianity? Do you think this is as good as it gets or you believe there is more to be discovered in God? Don't you agree with me that the Word of God on our lips as Christians should be producing more results than we currently experience? Then I call you to the place of intercession. Intercession for every Christian and the church. That God will work in us and cause us to return to His agenda of discipling nations for Him. I implore you to pray for this army that God shows us in Joel 2. That indeed the generals, lieutenants, and others He has been preparing (or need to prepare) will awake to the needs of God for this generation. That a fire be kindled in our hearts we can no longer ignore.

We need God to visit our church leaders. It is obvious that they would not listen to those of us who are "below" them. They have run for so many years on the tracks of religion that what we speak of now seems but like gibberish in their ears. I heard a leader of a major church denomination in Nigeria say once that "the easiest way to destroy whatever you are trying to say is for you to attempt as a follower to correct your leader". He was emphasizing in that message that no matter what your experiences have been with God, you cannot and should not ever attempt to point your leader in a direction you feel is correct. This is the sad situation we find ourselves in the Nigerian church. Our leaders do not believe this generation of preachers have anything to offer the church. But how can a man suddenly feel he has monopoly of

God? This is not how it was in the early church and I only wonder how we arrived at our own patterns ad standards.

Unfortunately, we cannot start an argument, revolution or war. Like I said earlier in the book, my goal with writing is not to dis church leadership or cause resentment within our denominations but to point us back to where we should be going in our dealings with God. I sincerely am hoping that as I have been stirred, you too have been provoked to shut yourself away from all the noise and activity until you find God or God finds you. Whichever one happens, the result is the same.

We can only go on our knees and cry for God to engage His sons and daughters who are our church leaders on these crucial matters. We cannot be unprepared for the next season in our lives as the church of the living God. For if we attempt to do so, we would be mortgaging the future of the generations coming behind us. In certain countries and continents of the world, Christianity suffered a massive blow (as I am suspecting will hit the church in Africa and Nigeria very soon) and they never recovered. So, you see pubs, bars and night clubs in buildings formerly owned by churches. People are in these buildings drinking and celebrating the prince of this world and yet the building has a massive cross standing on the roof. This is the only reminder that "God was once here". How sad it must be for those who lived before the major blow came. Now when they see this situation they can only wish they responded when God called them to intercession.

Religion and religious activity is a killer beloved reader. You do not attack this "spirit" with kid's gloves we must violently uproot it from our Christianity today otherwise the Nigerian church will be unprepared for what is coming next. All the "noise" we are making in our sanctuaries will soon be tested. And if all we have done is indoctrinate men to be better members of our church, then it would be a sad sight to behold when in the face of real life circumstances men cannot validate their so-called experiences with God.

We cannot continue to say men and women should not visit the shrines of native doctors, witch doctors or juju priests. We cannot continue to point at which man of God is fake or being used of the devil. We seem to be saying they are fake but every time some members of denominations (which we say is the real deal) contact them, these so called "fake prophets" can provide results. We must now hide ourselves in the secret place and cry to God for Him to return the kind of results experienced in the early church to our own Christianity in this generation or bend our head in shame and admit that juju priests, witch doctors, native doctors and false preachers have better results than us.

Unless we confront these anomalies and lack of tangible results in our gatherings, we cannot blame anyone for going where they believe "God is".

I am calling on everyone to honestly, sincerely and openly question the religious activity we are peddling in our various denominations. I know we have been told to keep our mouths shut but we cannot continue like this because we know what is ahead. A wise man said "all it takes for evil to thrive is for good men to do nothing" If you say it does not concern you, one day not too far from today you would regret your silence. I encourage us to begin to evaluate our meetings and gatherings. Anything that does not add value has become unnecessary. Let us clearly define what working for God is and focus on doing His work indeed. Nothing else would be acceptable.

A wise man said "the strength of the oppressor lies in the ignorance of the oppressed". With this I am not by any means concluding that what is happening in Christendom can be likened to oppression but I use to this to emphasize the fact that ignorance incapacitates a man regardless of whatever potentials available to him. To eliminate this possibility of ignorance in the church, God has helped me to set you on a journey with this book. I sincerely pray that we would all be drawn to the secret place with an open bible and hearts set on fire for the genuine manifestations of the supernatural. Our attitude should be one of resoluteness and earnestness. We would rather die than continue in this nominal Christian life. If God indeed has designed us to function in this realm as gods, then we must appropriate what is available and produce the results thereof.

There are deeper dimensions in God and this generation must be not become satisfied with standing on the periphery of what is possible. We must go deeper and experience the fullness of God.

I long for a church where our prayer meetings will be well attended because people know of a surety as we pray, there will be results. Our bible study meetings or services will be well attended because the Word of God being preached will be the truth of what Christ has made available for us by His death on the cross and be dividing asunder the soul and spirit, exposing the truth about each man to himself such that he goes home to cry for more of God's presence. That in our services the Holy Spirit will be given room to do what He wants to do in the lives of men. These and many more my heart craves for in the present-day church of God. God can do exceedingly, abundantly above all we ask or think so I trust Him for this miracle in the church.

May the church leader, worker, minister or member who reads this book feel the burden for revival and fall on their knees to cry to God for the manifestation of His glory in our denominations. What we call glory now is nowhere near what God wants to show the world through His church. The large auditoriums, the millions in attendance, the cars we drive or the size of our bank accounts is not all that God wants to do with His church. I feel God is desperately yearning for us to come up higher; to a place where He can become more visible in our midst. Men should walk into our auditoriums and without a shadow of doubt, know that we are blessed. The blessing should no longer be defined by what kind of car you drive, but how much of God you carry such that when a man says "I am blessed" we can tell by the manifest presence of God in the life of such a man. "He that hath my commandments, and keepeth them, he it is that loveth me: and he that loveth me shall be loved of my Father, and I will love him, and will manifest myself to him" John 14:21. This I believe is the next level God wants to take us to. Nothing less will be good enough for what is coming ahead.

There is more to God than what Christendom is currently experiencing and sharing with the world and He wants to use the church as a platform to reveal deeper dimensions of Himself to the world. Our passion should be to experience God so much so that men would desire to come into His family from the supernatural happenings in our own lives. There is no greater evangelistic tool than the proof of changed lives. No matter how many crusades we do, conventions we hold and camp meetings we gather in, nothing can influence the world greater than genuine proof of men who have encountered God and can show the world the results of such an encounter.

Situations are not going to test the cars we drive or the strengths of our mega and sophisticated structures. Neither will our air-conditioned auditoriums come under the scrutiny of the number one enemy of the church. The test would be to prove what we claim God has told us in His Word and the profession of our faith. If we go back to Genesis 3, we see the pattern clearly revealed. Satan comes and asks Eve "Has God said…?" The question had nothing to do with Eve's enjoyment of the garden or her love relationship with Adam. It was specific; what exactly has God told you? Can you now in this real situation validate your conviction on that Word?

Eve faced her own real test of her profession and we all know the result.

Ours is fast approaching and if we are not careful, when we come to our "Eve Moment" we might have the same results Eve and Adam did. Without having to belabour the issue, we all know the consequence suffered because of this seeming "simple" experience in the garden. To say there will be dire consequences for organized religion if and when we cannot validate our confessions in the face of real life situations, will be putting it mildly. The church may never be able to recover if this was to be the case.

Realize that when the test comes for the church in Africa and Nigeria, it would not select which denomination to attack. It will be an onslaught against all that we believe in and profess as Christians. Right this very moment as you are reading this is the best time for every one of us to rise as one regardless of our affiliations and call God to help His church prepare for the day of reckoning. This matter is one of choice and except God puts what I am sharing as burden in your heart, you might not be able to arise and work His works.

The thing about passion is, it cannot be faked. It is either you have it, or you don't.

This is an encouragement to all those who have become increasingly dissatisfied with organized religion in our present-day Christianity. You are not alone in how you are feeling deep inside. God has discomfited you for a reason; that you may arise and act to correct what is going wrong in Christendom. We will not correct this by fighting our leaders neither will we start a rebellion by breaking away from the family of God. Our response must be two-fold. We would pray and we would speak.

We pray because God still has power to change men. Scriptures say in *Proverbs 21:1 "the heart of a king is in the hand of the Lord and like a river He turns it wherever it pleases Him".* I am confident that the hearts of all those whom God Himself called to lead the church in this generation are still in His hands. There is no denying though that for some, their hearts have long since floated out of His hands into "other" hands. However, we pray that those whom He still holds and who also have not given their hearts to idols, the Lord Himself will begin to turn their hearts back to the pattern He showed us in His Word.

We would speak because faith without works is dead. Our praying must be followed up with purposeful actions. Whatever platform God has priviledged us to have, be it as a Sunday school teacher, Home Cell/House Fellowship Leader, Pastor, Classroom teacher, Doctor, Bus Driver, Cleaner, or whatever, we must keep preaching the truth. Christianity as we know it today is not where God expects it to be. We have too little results and there are a lot of frustrations within our buildings. God cannot just have chosen to "reduce" His influence on the world in our time. There must be something wrong; there must have been a time we deviated and left God behind. Except we go back and get things right we would continue to grow mega churches but very few authentic Christians.

We must insist that the Holy Spirit be given His rightful place in our denominations. He is the grace of God given to men to function as God expects us to function in the earthly realm. When one buys a car, he knows the car is expected to run on a certain fuel. If He chooses not to fuel the car, ultimately, he would have a useless box even though he calls it a car. God made sure He provided for us what we need. In fact, Jesus said "it is better for you that I go because as I go, I would send you another comforter to be with you" John 16:7. It seems to me Jesus was saying, "I have finished my own assignment. My assignment was to reveal the Father and show you how a child in our family can live supernaturally in the earthly realm. However, for you to produce these results, you need what I had and except I go you cannot get Him." No man can know the Father except there is an encounter with Jesus. Likewise, no man can truly know Jesus until there is an encounter with the Holy Spirit. It seems to me we do not understand what it actually means to be baptized with the Holy Spirit. The church in my day does not understand what it means to be full of the Spirit of God. If we can become conscious of this power dwelling in us, our influence amongst men would greatly increase.

Jesus was full of the God head. He was full of the Holy Spirit. For us to now attempt to do this work without the same baptism He enjoyed, it can only be described as an effort in futility. We need to call the church back to waiting upon God for the earnest baptism of the Holy Spirit. Only then can we with great power bear witness to the resurrection of Jesus Christ. It baffles me how we have chosen to neglect such an important aspect of our lives as Christians.

A man who had been diagnosed with tuberculosis and given a few days to live could not resist the burden God had put in his soul for the American Indians. So, while doctors were waiting for him to die he fell on his face crying to God "Oh Lord give me souls or take my soul". This man went on to not only live for many years but a fire of revival broke out amongst the American Indians. Beloved, it cannot be faked. Except God lights a fire in our souls we would continue to be satisfied with the mundane we are currently experiencing in modern day Christianity.

Oh, that all-over Nigeria and Africa, an earnestness be born in our hearts as we all cry for a fresh baptism of the Holy Spirit upon all Christians. That our prayer points shift from all the "mundane" things we have been asking for and we begin to ask the Father for a tremendous outpour of the Holy Spirit. The Word of God on our lips will become powerful again, our shadows will heal men on the streets, governments and nations will look to the church and her leadership for guidance and help, our influence will be restored and men indeed will walk in the supernatural.

Of their own accord, charlatans and false prophets will close shop and go and hide their heads in shame because there will be a clear distinction between them that know Him, and them that know Him not. Or better still, them that have been with Him and them that have not. The Spirit of God will by Himself draw a clear line for all the world to see. Just as it was in the days of Paul (Acts 19:14) where the sons of Sceva in an attempt to do what they had no authority to and were duly disgraced by the devil, so shall it be in our generation. We would no longer need to point fingers to identify who is fake and who is real. Men themselves will see the distinction as charlatans will be openly disgraced by not only demons and devils but real life circumstances.

Become a part of the supernatural generation and let us do exploits together. The times and seasons are obvious, all we need do is position ourselves correctly.

May God hear us as we pray and may He stretch forth His hands to validate the words we speak with sign and wonders that men may believe that a new dawn is upon the church.

A wise man said "Prayer is to the believer what capital is to the business man" without it brethren, our lives, church buildings and the world at large will be bankrupt of the supernatural.
Let us pray…

WHAT NOW?

*He who fears God fears no man.
He who kneels before God will stand in any situation.
A daily glimpse at the Holy One will find us subdued by His omnipresence, staggered by His omnipotence, silenced by His omniscience and solemnized by His holiness. His holiness will become our holiness. Holiness-teaching contradicted by unholy living is the bane of this hour. A holy minister is an awful weapon in the hand of God*
– Robert Murray McCheyne

Light yourself on fire with passion and people will come from miles to watch you burn
– John Wesley

Give me one hundred preachers who fear nothing but sin, and desire nothing but God, and I care not a straw whether they be clergymen or laymen; such alone will shake the gates of hell and set up the kingdom of heaven on Earth
– John Wesley

If Christianity continues on the present path, what will remain?
– Steve Hill

Final words...
We are in the last days... But the burden of these times seem to have eluded God's church. Oh, that we may look and see that the signs... Our Saviour's return draws near!

The Man Jesus Christ is the syllabus for the Christian journey. In studying Him we can be sure we would live accurately in this realm. Remember when that centurion stood at the foot of Christ's cross? He watched as our Saviour in agony cried out to His Father and yielded His Spirit and at that instant, the centurion's opinion of the Man on the cross changed. "Indeed, this was the Son of God!" Even in death, His life was still making impact.

"And when the centurion, which stood over against him, saw that he so cried out, and gave up the ghost, he said, Truly this man was the Son of God" Mark 15:39

What will be said of you beloved when your time here is called? When men analyze the way you lived and died, what will be said? What will be written in the scrolls of the Mighty One, the Judge of the whole earth when our Christianity is weighed on the scales? If we do nothing today, then how will we face our King?

You dear readers are the key to changing what we have experienced so far in Christendom. I wish like Wesley you would shut yourself in the secret place of prayer and catch some fire so you can start a revival in your denomination, community or city. Yes, there will be resistance, there will be hard times, you might even be ostracized but you must not be deterred. The New Testament experience is the standard for the church. Anything less is not correct!

Young or old, rich or poor, eloquent or not, we must all arise and pound heaven's door till God responds to us on this matter. The kingdom of God is at hand!

The deepest needs of the hour are a fresh outpouring of the Holy Spirit and a release of the burden of the Lord into our hearts. Our generation lacks a sense of responsibility. We think all Christianity is, is to make us comfortable in this life and in addition, especially in the Nigerian church, to kill all our enemies. Beloved, there is more to the Christian faith and except we be endued with power from on high and we begin to carry the burden of responsibility, we would have no impact whatsoever on our world. We would grow larger auditoriums, drive limousines and eat in the best restaurants but the souls of men will be asked at our hands when we appear before the Monarch of the Universe. Christians must begin to live like sent men. This is what John the Baptist understood that drove him to wilderness, changed his natural appetites and chose his garment. When his contemporaries where feasting, marrying and "wearing the best

Italian suits", his meal was locusts and wild honey and his garment camel skin yet he was "comfortable" and stayed in that wilderness till the day of his showing (manifestation or unveiling) to Israel. "And the child grew, and waxed strong in spirit, and was in the deserts till the day of his shewing unto Israel" Luke 1:80. His secret is revealed in John 1:6 "There was a man sent from God, whose name was John" John understood he was a sent man and could not bear to live carelessly in opposition to the One who sent him. The Christians of old understood this and we see how unlearned men and women conquered Rome, outliving persecution, sacrificing their lives, spreading the good news and establishing Christianity. Church history is replete with stories of the Monrovians, The Quakers and others who understood that there were sent men.

I wish that when we are gone, it will be written as it was written for John the Baptist, "There was a man sent from God whose name was… Or There was a woman sent from God whose name was…

Beloved, you've been sent; shot as an arrow from the Master's hand to that establishment, school, government or country. The question is, do you know that you are sent? If that sense of responsibility does not come upon you, you will pursue salary, promotions, good grades and the accolades of men while the fulfilment of God's assignment suffers. The thing about God is, when men fail He can raise other men or even stones. May we arise again and begin to ask – Where is the burden of the Lord? A Christian without a burden or sense of responsibility will be useless to God's agenda in these last days.

Will you again waste your time and energies in meetings that have no proof of God's presence? Will you allow yourself to be just a worker in a denomination while the true work of God suffers? Will you be satisfied with the abnormal Christian life? Are you willing to take risks and step out by faith? These questions must tug at our hearts and let us not alone until we provide answers with the way we live our lives on a daily basis.

The bible is very clear on what the pattern is. Jesus did not hide the heart of the Father from us; He even gave us the Holy Spirit so we can be led into all truth about what He wants from us. We cannot then sit back and allow traditions and laws of men to inhibit the flow of the Spirit in our generation.

There is so much going on in our denominations and Christian circles that are a complete waste of time; mere celebration of carnality. I encourage you to begin to ask why? To what end are some of the things we do? Why do we do rallies across town with speakers blaring, convoys full of people and all the other "drama" while the people we claim we are trying to reach (or should I say invite) have to get stuck in hold-ups and traffic jams because we have blocked the roads in the name of us advertising a programme? Would Jesus have done this? What exactly are we trying to achieve? To what end is most of the activity we do in Christendom today? To what end? These are hard questions that church-people will not want to address. But like I said at the beginning of this book, this is not about becoming popular or accepted this is about finding relief for my burdened heart. We must begin to ask questions so we can maximize the Christian life. I refuse to believe that this was all God left us here to do. If by the slightest chance, Christianity as it is today is all that this new creation life offers then with all humility and sincerity, I would want none of it. The reason I press on is because deep down the voice of the Holy Spirit rings "There is more and if you can break free from the religious shackles you can drink from the wells of life and fountain of living waters" This, I believe we all must desire to do in this generation.

I pray that we all approach God with strong crying and tears and demand that His glory be restored to the church no matter the cost. If we were to have smaller auditoriums but better men He can use, may it be so. If the world were to call us fanatics but not be able to argue with our proofs, may it be so. If we would separate ourselves from the love of positions and titles and become open to criticism that the awe and fear of the people may return to the church, then may it be so. We would rather have it so than continue in this powerless Christianity. My generation cannot be remembered as a powerless generation no not on our watch.

How seriously beloved are you looking upon the things God has called you to do? Are you applying your life to it? What exactly are you applying your life to? What is consuming your time? What has captured your heart? What is driving your life? Can it be said that you are truly, sincerely and genuinely living for the Master?

There must be something that heaven must credit to your life because your life was accurate! Enough of mediocre Christian living... It is time to press in and go far with God!

"There is life more abundant – the life of POWER! The life of real satisfaction. The life of knowing that your living has not been in vain! Surely it is worth every sacrifice to know that we have followed in the steps of the Son of God" A.A. Allen

I have determined dear soldier of Christ that my life will not be a waste. We must not live useless lives, enjoy a meaningless existence and die worthless deaths. God must find our lives a platform for which to express Himself with great grace and power in this generation. Nothing in life is as important as doing for God what He ordained that you accomplish for Him from the time of your birth. I have mentioned earlier that a purposeless life is a useless life. Can there be something in your heart that burns as fuel for your life and that you are also willing to die for? I believe that the more Christians who come to this point in their walk with God, the greater increase in the manifestations of the supernatural we shall begin to see.

Until then, I retire again to my secret place to cry for my own life. Oh God, please work your work in my heart and life that I too may indeed become an authentic instrument in your hand. For me, the church and my generation. I trust God that by the time some of you holding this book in your hand would be reading this, God would have responded with supernatural proofs to the cries of all His children for a fresh revival in Christendom.

May organized religion be expunged from the church forever in Jesus name! May we have structures that create better men for Jesus and not ones that enslave and celebrate the abuse of the Christian faith. May honour return to the church as we raise men who are indeed living proofs of the Word of God. If we say God can heal, may healings happen outside our denominational buildings. If we say God is powerful, may power be seen and felt in our nations. If we say we are believers, then may signs and wonders begin to follow us as Jesus said will follow them that believe. Otherwise, may we stay on our knees in our secret place until we see it all happen!

Enough of religion and religious activity!

Also Available - Inspiring Book by
Kesiena Henry Esiri, Jr.
NAKED FLESH

Also Available - Inspiring Book by Kesiena Henry Esiri, Jr.

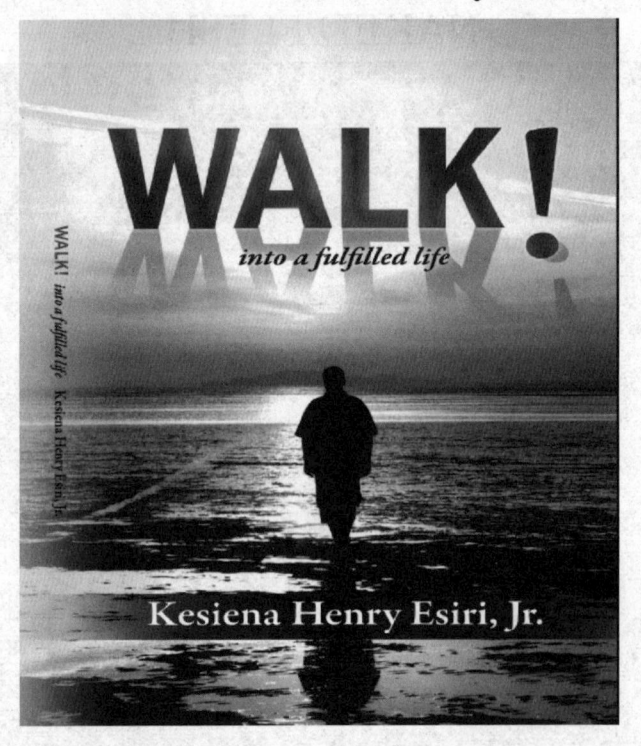

"Arise, take up thy bed and walk! John 5:8 (KJV) Everyone might not get the opportunity of an education, the opportunity of wealthy parents, or even the opportunity of a great job. Nevertheless, we all will always get the opportunity to come to the realization that we can make it if we draw a picture of our future and determine to take a step a day towards living the dream.... This book is designed to exhort, encourage and challenge you to become a better you. It is a prophetic declaration to you that it is your time to arise and walk. Receive Illumination and Revelation; break free from strongholds; release your potentials, and WALK into a fulfilled life." *If you are yearning for something extraordinary and worthwhile in life, then order and read this book!*

www.facebook.com/PastorKesiena
@KesienaEsiri